FRENCH

in 10 minutes a day®

P9-CED-573

by Kristine Kershul, M.A., University of California, Santa Barbara

Consultants: Jan Fisher Brousseau   Hagar Shirman
Susan Worthington

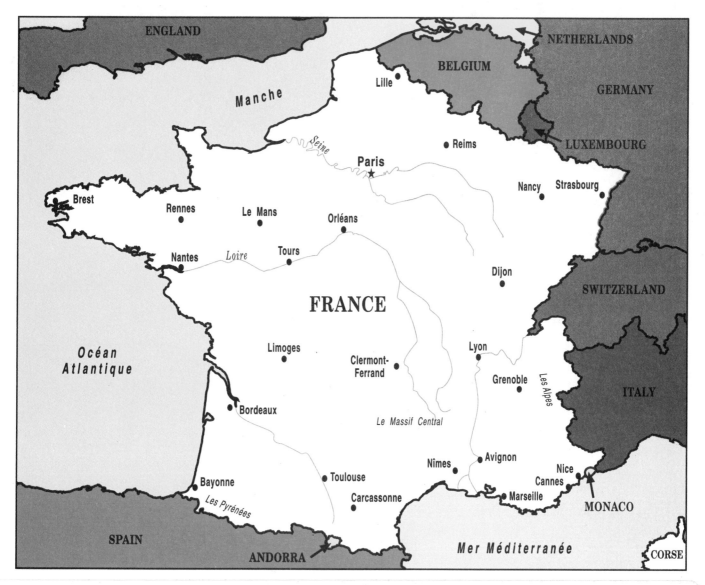

Bilingual Books, Inc.
1719 West Nickerson Street, Seattle, WA 98119
Tel: (206) 284-4211 Fax: (206) 284-3660

www.10minutesaday.com • www.bbks.com

ISBN: 978-1-931873-02-4   Second printing, May 2010

Can you say this?

(kess)　　　　*(kuh)*　　*(say)*
Qu'est-ce que c'est?
what is　　　　　　　　　　　that

(say)　　*(tewn)*　　*(fluhr)*
C'est une fleur.
it is　　　　a　　　flower

(zhuh)　*(voo-dray)*　　　*(ewn)*　　*(fluhr)*
Je voudrais une fleur.
I　　would like　　　　a　　　flower

If you can say this, you can learn to speak French. You will be able to easily order wine, lunch, theater tickets, pastry, or anything else you wish. With your best French accent, you simply ask **"Qu'est-ce que c'est?"** *(kess) (kuh) (say)* and, upon learning what it is, you can order it with **"Je voudrais ça,"** *(zhuh) (voo-dray) (sah)*. Sounds easy, doesn't it?

The purpose of this book is to give you an **immediate** speaking ability in French. French is the leading language not only in France, but in parts of Switzerland, Belgium, Canada and numerous countries in Africa too. French is a language of beautiful sounds. To help you master these sounds, this book offers a unique and easy system of pronunciation above each word which walks you through learning French.

If you are planning a trip or moving to where French is spoken, you will be leaps ahead of everyone if you take just a few minutes a day to learn the easy key words that this book offers. Start with Step 1 and don't skip around. Each day work as far as you can comfortably go in those 10 minutes. Don't overdo it. Some days you might want to just review. If you forget a word, you can always look it up in the glossary. Spend your first 10 minutes studying the map on the previous page. And yes, have fun learning your new language.

As you work through the Steps, always use the special features which only this series offers. This book contains sticky labels and flash cards, free words, puzzles and quizzes. When you have completed this book, cut out the menu guide and take it along on your trip.

(lahl-fah-bay)
L'Alphabet
the alphabet

Throughout this book you will find an an easy pronunciation guide above all new words. Refer to this Step whenever you need help, but remember, spend no longer than 10 minutes a day.

Most letters in French are identical to those in English and are pronounced in just the same way.

(b)	(d)	(f)	(k)	(l)	(m)	(n)	(p)	(t)	(v)	(z)
b	**d**	**f**	**k**	**l**	**m**	**n**	**p**	**t**	**v**	**z**

Here is a guide to help you learn the sounds of the French letters which are pronounced somewhat differently. Practice these sounds with the examples given which are mostly towns or areas in France you might wish to visit. You can always refer back to these pages if you need to review.

French letter	English sound	Examples	Write it here
a, à, â	ah	**Paris** (pah-ree)	Paris, Paris, Paris
ai	ay	**Calais** (kah-lay)	Calais, Calais, Calais
au, eau	oh	**Bordeaux** (bor-doh)	Bordeaux, Bordeaux, Bordeaux
(before a,o,u) **c**	k	**Colmar** (kohl-mar)	Colmar, Colmar, Colmar
(elsewhere) **c**	s	**Nice** (nees)	Nice, Nice, Nice
ç	s	**Alençon** (ah-lah$^{(n)}$-soh$^{(n)}$)	Alençon, Alençon, Alençon
ch	sh	**Champagne** (shah$^{(n)}$-pahn-yuh)	Champagne, Champagne, Champagne
e	(as in let) eh	**Montpellier** (moh$^{(n)}$-pel-yay)	Montpellier, Montpellier, Montpellier
	uh	**Le Havre** (luh)(ah-vruh)	Le Havre, Le Havre, Le Havre
è, ê, ei	(as in let) eh	**la Seine** (lah)(sen)	la Seine, la Seine, la Seine
é	ay	**Orléans** (or-lay-ah$^{(n)}$)	Orléans, Orléans, Orléans
(before a,o,u) **g**	g	**Garonne** (gar-ohn)	Garonne, Garonne, Garonne
(before e,i,y) **g**	zh	**Gironde** (zhee-rohnd)	Gironde, Gironde, Gironde
gn	(as in onion) n-y	**Avignon** (ah-veen-yoh$^{(n)}$)	Avignon, Avignon, Avignon
h	always silent	**Honfleur** (oh$^{(n)}$-fluhr)	Honfleur, Honfleur, Honfleur
i	ee	**Lille** (leel)	Lille, Lille, Lille
(before e,i,y) **j**	zh	**Le Jura** (luh)(zhew-rah)	Le Jura, Le Jura, Le Jura
o	oh	**Limoges** (lee-mohzh)	Limoges, Limoges, Limoges
oi	wah	**Poitiers** (pwah-tee-ay)	Poitiers, Poitiers, Poitiers
ou, oû	oo	**Tours** (toor)	Tours, Tours, Tours

Letter	Sound	Example	*Write it here*
qu	k	**Q**uimper *(ka$^{(n)}$-pair)*	Quimper
r	r *(slightly rolled)*	**R**ennes *(ren)*	Rennes
s	s	**S**tra**s**bourg *(strahs-boor)*	Strasbourg
s *(between vowels)*	z	Toulou**s**e *(too-looz)*	Toulouse
u	ew/oo *(with your lips rounded)*	Tourn**u**s *(toor-new)*	Tournus
w	v	Rique**w**ihr *(ree-kuh-veer)*	Riquewihr
x	ks	Lu**x**embourg *(lewk-sah$^{(n)}$-boor)*	Luxembourg
	gz	A**x**iat *(ah-gzee-ah)*	Axiat
	s	Bru**x**elles *(brew-sel)*	Bruxelles
y	ee	L**y**on *(lee-oh$^{(n)}$)*	Lyon

In addition to the sounds above, French has many nasal vowel sounds. Whenever you see the small elevated $^{(n)}$, think nasal!

Letter	Sound	Example	*Write it here*
am, an, em, en	*(taunt nasalized)* ah$^{(n)}$	**Am**boise *(ah$^{(n)}$-bwahz)*	Amboise
		Ca**en** *(kah-ah$^{(n)}$)*	Caen
im, in, aim, ain, eim, ein	*(than nasalized)* a$^{(n)}$	St.-Sav**in** *(sa$^{(n)}$-sah-va$^{(n)}$)*	St.-Savin
		S**ain**tes *(sa$^{(n)}$t)*	Saintes
		R**eim**s *(ra$^{(n)}$s)*	Reims
om, on	*(don't nasalized)* oh$^{(n)}$	Toul**on** *(too-loh$^{(n)}$)*	Toulon
um, un	*(fun nasalized)* uh$^{(n)}$	Mel**un** *(mel-uh$^{(n)}$)*	Melun
-tion	*(as in station)* syoh$^{(n)}$	Atten**tion**! *(ah-tah$^{(n)}$-syoh$^{(n)}$)*	Attention

Just as in English, "q" is always joined with the letter "u." The letter "u" is then silent.

Note that when many French words begin with a vowel they are joined together in their pronunciation with the previous word. This liaison is a key part of French pronunciation.

(voo) *(ah-vay)*
vous + **avez** becomes *(voo)* *(zah-vay)* **vous avez**

(say) *(ewn)* *(fluhr)*
c'est une fleur becomes *(say)* *(tewn)* *(fluhr)* **c'est une fleur**

Sometimes the phonetics may seem to contradict your pronunciation guide. Don't panic! The easiest and best possible phonetics have been chosen for each individual word. Pronounce the phonetics just as you see them. Don't over-analyze them. Speak with a French accent and, above all, enjoy yourself!

When you arrive in **France**, *(frah⁽ⁿ⁾s)* **Québec** *(kay-bek)* or another French-speaking country, the very first thing you will need to do is ask questions — "Where **(où)** *(oo)* is the bus stop?" "**Où** *(oo)* can I exchange money?" "**Où** is the lavatory?" "**Où** is a restaurant?" "**Où** do I catch a taxi?" "**Où** is a good hotel?" "**Où** is my luggage?" — and the list will go on and on for the entire length of your visit. In French, there are SEVEN KEY QUESTION WORDS to learn. For example, the seven key question words will help you find out exactly what you are ordering in a restaurant before you order it — and not after the surprise (or shock!) arrives. Notice that only one letter is different in the French words for "what" and "who." Don't confuse them! Take a few minutes to study and practice saying the seven key question words listed below. Then cover the French with your hand and fill in each of the blanks with the matching **mot** *(moh)* **français.** *(frah⁽ⁿ⁾-say)*

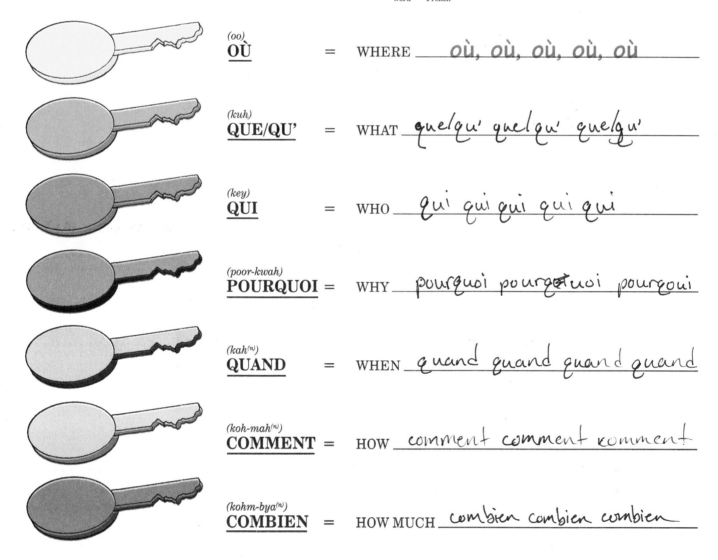

(oo)
OÙ = WHERE _où, où, où, où, où_

(kuh)
QUE/QU' = WHAT _quelqu' quelqu' quelqu'_

(key)
QUI = WHO _qui qui qui qui qui_

(poor-kwah)
POURQUOI = WHY _pourquoi pourquoi pourqoui_

(kah⁽ⁿ⁾)
QUAND = WHEN _quand quand quand quand_

(koh-mah⁽ⁿ⁾)
COMMENT = HOW _comment comment comment_

(kohm-bya⁽ⁿ⁾)
COMBIEN = HOW MUCH _combien combien combien_

Now test yourself to see if you really can keep these **mots** *(moh)* / words straight in your mind. Draw lines between the French **et** *(ay)* / and English equivalents below.

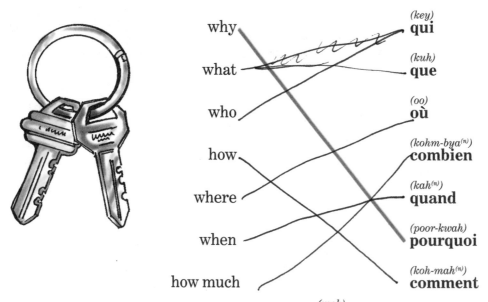

why	**qui** *(key)*
what	**que** *(kuh)*
who	**où** *(oo)*
how	**combien** *(kohm-bya⁽ⁿ⁾)*
where	**quand** *(kah⁽ⁿ⁾)*
when	**pourquoi** *(poor-kwah)*
how much	**comment** *(koh-mah⁽ⁿ⁾)*

Examine the following questions containing these **mots** *(moh)*. Practice the sentences out loud **et** *(ay)* / and then practice by copying the French in the blanks underneath each question.

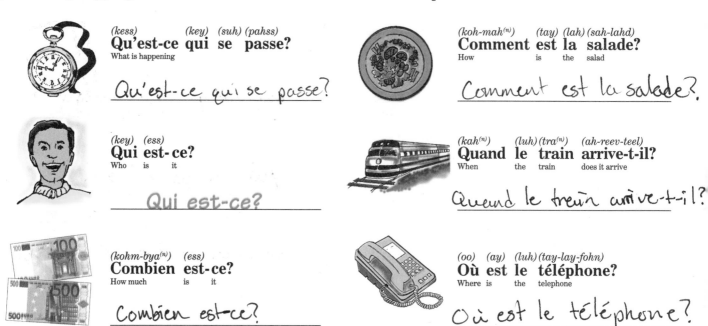

(kess) (key) (suh) (pahss)
Qu'est-ce qui se passe?
What is happening

Qu'est-ce qui se passe?

(koh-mah⁽ⁿ⁾) (tay) (lah) (sah-lahd)
Comment est la salade?
How   is   the   salad

Comment est la salade?

(key) (ess)
Qui est-ce?
Who   is   it

Qui est-ce?

(kah⁽ⁿ⁾) (luh) (tra⁽ⁿ⁾) (ah-reev-teel)
Quand le train arrive-t-il?
When   the   train   does it arrive

Quand le train arrive-t-il?

(kohm-bya⁽ⁿ⁾) (ess)
Combien est-ce?
How much   is   it

Combien est-ce?

(oo) (ay) (luh) (tay-lay-fohn)
Où est le téléphone?
Where is   the   telephone

Où est le téléphone?

"**Où**" *(oo)* will be your most used question **mot** *(moh)*. Say each of the following French sentences aloud. Then write out each sentence without looking at the example. If you don't succeed on the first try, don't give up. Just practice each sentence until you are able to do it easily. Remember "**qu**" is pronounced like "k" and "**est-ce**" is pronounced "ess."

(soh⁽ⁿ⁾) *(lay)* *(twah-let)*
Où sont les toilettes?

(oo) *(ay)* *(luh)* *(tahx-ee)*
Où est le taxi?
where is the taxi

(oo) *(ay)* *(loh-toh-boos)*
Où est l'autobus?
where is bus

Où sont les toilettes?

Où est le taxi?

Où est l'autobus?

(ay) *(luh)* *(reh-stoh-rah⁽ⁿ⁾)*
Où est le restaurant?

(lah) *(bah⁽ⁿ⁾k)*
Où est la banque?
the bank

(ay) *(loh-tel)*
Où est l'hôtel?
hotel

Où est le restaurant?

Où est la banque?

Où est l'hôtel?

(wee)
Oui, you can see similarities between **anglais** and **français** if you look closely. You will be
yes   *(ah⁽ⁿ⁾-glay)* English   *(frah⁽ⁿ⁾-say)* French

(moh)
amazed at the number of **mots** which are identical (or almost identical) in both languages. Of
words

course, they do not always sound the same when spoken by a French speaker, but the

(see-mee-lar-ee-tay) *(ay)*
similarités will certainly surprise you **et** make your work here easier. Listed below are five
similarities   and

(ah) *(ay)*
"free" **mots** beginning with " **a** " to help you get started. Be sure to say each **mot** aloud **et** then

(frah⁽ⁿ⁾-say)
write out the **mot français** in the blank to the right.

☑	l'accident *(lahk-see-dah⁽ⁿ⁾)*	accident	*l'accident, l'accident, l'accident*
☑	l'addition *(lah-dee-syoh⁽ⁿ⁾)*	the bill in a restaurant	*l'addition, l'addition, l'addition*
☑	l'admission *(lahd-mee-syoh⁽ⁿ⁾)*	admission **a**	*l'admission, l'admission, l'admission*
☑	l'adresse *(lah-dress)*	address	*l'adresse, l'adresse, l'adresse*
☑	aidez-moi! *(ay-day-mwah)*	aid me! help me!	*aidez-moi, aidez-moi, aidez-moi*

Free **mots** like these will appear at the bottom of the following pages in a yellow color band.

They are easy — enjoy them! Remember, in French, the letter **"h"** is silent.

7

(frah⁽ⁿ⁾-say)
Le français has multiple **mots** for "the," "a," and "some," but they are very easy.
French (language)   words

(luh)	*(lah)*	*(l)*	*(lay)*	*(uh⁽ⁿ⁾)*	*(ewn)*	*(dew)*	*(duh) (lah)*	*(duh) (l)*	*(day)*
le	**la**	**l'**	**les**	**un**	**une**	**du**	**de la**	**de l'**	**des**
the	the	the	the	a	a	some	some	some	some

(gar-soh⁽ⁿ⁾)
le garçon
the boy

(gar-soh⁽ⁿ⁾)
les garçons
the boys

(fee-yuh)
la fille
the girl

(fee-yuh)
les filles
the girls

(lohm)
l'homme
the man

(lay) (zohm)
les hommes
the men

(dew) (soo-kruh)
du sucre
some sugar

(duh) (lah) (moo-tard)
de la moutarde
some mustard

(ewn) (fahm)
une femme
a woman

(day) (fahm)
des femmes
some women

(uh) (nohm)
un homme
a man

(day) (zohm)
des hommes
some men

This might appear difficult, but only because it is different from **anglais.** *(ah⁽ⁿ⁾-glay)* Just remember you will be understood whether you say "**la fille** *(fee-yuh)*" or "**le fille.**" Soon you will automatically select the right one without even thinking about it.

In Step 2 you were introduced to the Seven Key QuestionWords. These seven words are the basics, the most essential building blocks for learning French. Throughout this book you will come across keys asking you to fill in the missing question word. Use this opportunity not only to fill in the blank on that key, but to review all your question words. Play with the new sounds, speak slowly and have fun.

☑	**l'alcool** *(lahl-kohl)*	alcohol	
☑	**les Alpes** *(lay) (zahlp)*	the Alps	
☑	**américain** *(ah-may-ree-ka⁽ⁿ⁾)*	American	**a**
☑	**l'animal** *(lah-nee-mahl)*	animal	
☑	**l'appartement** *(lah-par-teh-mah⁽ⁿ⁾)*	apartment	

l'alcool, l'alcool, l'alcool
les Alpes, les Alpes, les Alpes
américain, américain, américain
l'animal, l'animal, l'animal
l'appartement, l'appartement, l'appartement

4 Look Around You

Before you proceed **avec** *(ah-vek)* (with) this Step, situate yourself comfortably in your living room. Now look around you. Can you name the things that you see in this **pièce** *(pyess)* (room) in French? You can probably guess **la lampe** *(lahmp)* (lamp) and maybe even **la chaise.** *(shehz)* (chair) Let's learn the rest of them. After practicing these **mots** out loud, write them in the blanks below.

la fenêtre *(fuh-net-ruh)*
window

la lampe *(lahmp)* lamp	la lampe, la lampe
le canapé *(kah-nah-pay)* sofa	le canapé, le canapé
la chaise *(shehz)* chair	la chaise, la chaise
le tapis *(tah-pee)* carpet	le tapis, le tapis
la table *(tah-bluh)* table	la table, la table
la porte *(port)* door	la porte, la porte
la pendule *(pah(n)-dewl)* clock	la pendule, la pendule
le rideau *(ree-doh)* curtain	le rideau, le rideau
le téléphone *(tay-lay-fohn)* telephone	le téléphone, le téléphone

le tableau *(tah-bloh)* picture — le tableau, le tableau

You will notice that the correct form of **le**, **la** or **les** is given **avec** *(ah-vek)* (with) each noun. This tells you whether the noun is masculine (**le**) or feminine (**la**). Now open your book to the sticky labels on page 17 and later on page 35. Peel off the first 11 labels **et** *(ay)* proceed around the **pièce** *(pyess)* (room), labeling these items in your home. This will help to increase your French **mot** (word) power easily. Don't forget to say each **mot** as you attach the label.

Now ask yourself, **"Où est la lampe?"** *(lahmp)* **et** point at it while you answer, **"Voilà** *(vwah-lah)* (there is) **la lampe."**

Continue on down the list above until you feel comfortable with these new **mots**.

☑	**l'appétit** *(lah-pay-tee)*	appetite	l'appétit, l'appétit l'appétit
☑	**l'arrêt** *(lah-ray)*	stop, arrest	l'arrêt, l'arrêt l'arrêt
☑	**l'arrivée** *(lah-ree-vay)*	arrival	l'arrivée, l'arrivée, l'arrivée
☑	**l'attention** *(lah-tah(n)-syoh(n))*	attention	l'attention, l'attention, l'attention
☑	**l'auteur** *(loh-tur)*	author	l'auteur, l'auteur, l'auteur

a

9

(lah) (may-zoh⁽ⁿ⁾)
la maison = the house

(vwah-lah)   (may-zoh⁽ⁿ⁾)
Voilà la maison.
there is   house

(bew-roh)
le bureau
office

(sahl) (duh) (ba⁽ⁿ⁾)
la salle de bains
bathroom

(kwee-zeen)
la cuisine
kitchen

(shah⁽ⁿ⁾-bruh) (ah)(koo-shay)
la chambre à coucher
bedroom

(sahl)   (ah) (mah⁽ⁿ⁾-zhay)
la salle à manger
dining room

(lee-veeng-room)   (sah-loh⁽ⁿ⁾)
le living-room/le salon
living room

(gah-rahzh)
le garage
garage

(soo-sohl)
le sous-sol
basement

While learning these new **mots,** let's not forget:
(moh)
words

(loh-toh)   (vwah-tewr)
l'auto / la voiture
automobile, car

(moh-toh)   (moh-toh-see-klet)
la moto / la motocyclette
motorcycle

(vay-loh)   (bee-see-klet)
le vélo / la bicyclette
bicycle

l'auto / la voiture

la moto / la motocyclette

le vélo / la bicyclette

☑	**le balcon** *(bahl-koh⁽ⁿ⁾)*	balcony	*le balcon, le balcon, le balcon*
☑	**le ballon** *(bah-loh⁽ⁿ⁾)*	balloon, big ball	*le ballon, le ballon, le ballon*
☑	**la banane** *(bah-nahn)*	banana	*la banane la, la banane, la banane*
☑	**le banc** *(bah⁽ⁿ⁾)*	bench	*le banc, le banc, le banc*
☑	**la banque** *(bah⁽ⁿ⁾k)*	bank	*la banque, la banque, la banque*

b

10

(shah)
le chat
cat

(zhar-da⁽ⁿ⁾)
le jardin
garden

(fluhr)
les fleurs
flowers

le chat, le chat

le jardin, le jardin

les fleurs, les fleurs

(shya⁽ⁿ⁾)
le chien
dog

(bwaht) (oh) (let-ruh)
la boîte aux lettres
mailbox

(koo-ree-ay)
le courrier
mail

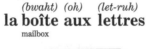

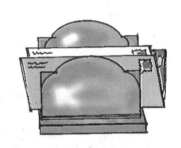

le chien, le chien

la boîte aux lettres

le courrier, le courrier

Peel off the next set of labels **et** _(ay)_ wander through your **maison** _(may-zoh⁽ⁿ⁾)_ learning these new **mots**. It will be somewhat difficult to label **le chat, les fleurs ou le chien,** _(shah) (fluhr) (oo) (shya⁽ⁿ⁾)_ but be creative. Practice by asking yourself, **"Où est l'auto?"** _(loh-toh)_ and reply, **"Voilà l'auto."** _(vwah-lah) (loh-toh)_

cat   flowers   or   dog   car   there is

Où est la maison? _(may-zoh⁽ⁿ⁾)_

☑	**le bifteck** _(beef-tek)_	beefsteak	_le bifteck, le bifteck, le bifteck_
☑	**le biscuit** _(bee-skwee)_	cookie	_le biscuit, le biscuit, le biscuit_
☑	**la bouteille** _(boo-tay)_	bottle	_la bouteille, la bouteille, la bouteille_
☑	**bref** _(brehf)_	brief, short	_bref, bref, bref_
☑	**brillant** _(bree-yah⁽ⁿ⁾)_	brilliant, sparkling	_brillant, billant, brillant_

b

11

(uh⁽ⁿ⁾) *(duh)* *(twah)*
Un, Deux, Trois!
one   two   three

Consider for a minute how important numbers are. How could you tell someone your phone

(oo)
number, your address **ou** your hotel room if you had no numbers? And think of how difficult it
or

(oo)
would be if you could not understand the time, the price of a croissant **ou** the correct bus to take.

(nohm-bruh)
When practicing the **nombres** below, notice the similarities which have been underlined for you
numbers

(wheat)   *(deez-wheat)*   *(set)*   *(deez-set)*
between **huit** and **dix-huit,** **sept** and **dix-sept,** **et** so on.
eight   eighteen   seven   seventeen

0 *(zay-roh)* **zéro**	zéro, zéro, zéro	
1 *(uh⁽ⁿ⁾)* **un**	un, un, un	
2 *(duh)* **deux**	deux, deux, deux	
3 *(twah)* **trois**	trois, trois, trois	
4 *(kah-truh)* **quatre**	quatre, quatre, quatre	
5 *(sank)* **cinq**	cinq, cinq, cinq	
6 *(seess)* **six**	six, six, six	
7 *(set)* **sept**	sept, sept, sept	
8 *(wheat)* **huit**	huit, huit, huit	
9 *(nuf)* **neuf**	neuf, neuf, neuf	
10 *(deess)* **dix**	dix, dix, dix	

10 *(deess)* **dix**	dix, dix, dix	
11 *(oh⁽ⁿ⁾z)* **onze**	onze, onze, onze	
12 *(dooz)* **douze**	douze, douze, douze	
13 *(trehz)* **treize**	treize, treize, treize	
14 *(kah-torz)* **quatorze**	quatorze, quatorze, quator	
15 *(ka⁽ⁿ⁾z)* **quinze**	quinze, quinze, quinze	
16 *(sehz)* **seize**	seize, seize, seize	
17 *(deez-set)* **dix-sept**	dix-sept, dix-sept, dix-sept	
18 *(deez-wheat)* **dix-huit**	dix-huit, dix-huit, dix-huit	
19 *(deez-nuf)* **dix-neuf**	dix-neuf, dix-neuf, dix-neuf	
20 *(va⁽ⁿ⁾)* **vingt**	vingt, vingt, vingt	

☑ **la capitale** *(kah-pee-tahl)* . . . . capital   la capitale, la capitale, la capitale
☑ **la cathédrale** *(kah-tay-drahl)* . . . . cathedral   la cathédrale, la cathédrale, la cathédrale
☑ **le cendrier** *(sah⁽ⁿ⁾-dree-ay)* . . . . ashtray   **c**   le cendrier, le cendrier, le cendrier
☑ **le centre** *(sah⁽ⁿ⁾-truh)* . . . . center   le centre, le centre, le centre
☐ **le champagne** *(shah⁽ⁿ⁾-pahn-yuh)* . . . . champagne   le champagne, le champagne, le champagne

(ew-tee-lee-zay)
Utilisez these **nombres** on a daily basis. Count to yourself *(ah(n))* **en français** when you brush your
use   numbers   in   French

teeth, exercise **ou** commute to work. Fill in the blanks below according to the *(nohm-bruh)* **nombres** given in
(oo)   numbers

parentheses. Now is also a good time to learn these two very important phrases.

(zhuh) (voo-dray)
je voudrais   *je voudrais, je voudrais, je voudrais*
I   would like

(noo) (voo-dree-oh(n))
nous voudrions   *nous voudrions, nous voudrions, nous voudrions*
we   would like

(zhuh) (voo-dray)
Je voudrais _____un_____   *(kart) (poh-stahl)* **carte postale.**   *(kohm-bya(n))* **Combien?** _____un_____
I   would like   (1)   postcard   how many   (1)

Je voudrais _____sept_____   *(ta(n)-bruh)* **timbres.**   **Combien?** _____sept_____
         (7)   stamps   (7)

Je voudrais _____huit_____   **timbres.**   **Combien?** _____huit_____
         (8)   stamps   (8)

Je voudrais _____cinq_____   **timbres.**   **Combien?** _____cinq_____
         (5)   (5)

(noo) (voo-dree-oh(n))
Nous voudrions _____neuf_____   *(kart) (poh-stahl)* **cartes postales.**   **Combien?** _____neuf_____
we   (9)   postcards   (9)

Nous voudrions _____dix_____   **cartes postales.**   **Combien?** _____dix_____
we   (10)   (10)

(zhuh)
Je voudrais _____un_____   *(tee-kay) (doh-toh-boos)* **ticket d'autobus.**   **Combien?** _____un_____
         (1)   ticket   (1)

Nous voudrions _____quatre_____   *(tee-kay)* **tickets.**   **Combien?** _____quatre_____
         (4)   tickets   (4)

Nous voudrions _____onze_____   **tickets.**   **Combien?** _____onze_____
         (11)   (11)

(voo-dray)
Je voudrais _____trois_____   *(tahs) (duh) (tay)* **tasses de thé.**   **Combien?** _____trois_____
         (3)   cups   of   tea   (3)

Nous voudrions _____quatre_____   *(vair) (doh)* **verres d'eau.**   **Combien?** _____quatre_____
         (4)   glasses   of   water   (how many)   (4)

☑ **le changement** *(shah(n)-zhuh-mah(n))* . . . . change   *le changement, le changement, le changement*
☑ **le chèque** *(shek)* . . . . bank check   *le chèque, le chèque, le chèque*
☑ **le chocolat** *(shoh-koh-lah)* . . . . chocolate   **C**   *le chocolat, le chocolat, le chocolat*
☑ **le coiffeur** *(kwah-fur)* . . . . hairdresser   *le coiffeur, le coiffeur, le coiffeur*
☐ **la communication** *(koh-mew-nee-kah-syoh(n))* . . . . communication   *la communication, la communication, la communication*

13

Now see if you can translate the following thoughts into **français.** *(lay)* **Les** *(ray-poh⁽ⁿ⁾s)* **réponses** are provided

French answers

upside down at the bottom of the *(pahzh)* **page.**

page

1. I would like seven postcards.

   Je voudrais sept carte postale.

2. I would like nine stamps.

   Je voudrais neuf timbres.

3. We would like four cups of tea.

   Nous voudrions quatre tasses de thé.

4. We would like three bus tickets.

   Nous voudrions trois tickets d'autobus.

Review **les nombres** 1 *(ah)* **à** 20. Write out your telephone number, fax number *(ay)* **et** cellular number.

to

Then write out a friend's telephone number and a relative's telephone number.

(2	0	6)	3	4	0	—	4	4	2	2
deux	zéro	six	trois	quatre	zéro		quatre	quatre	deux	deux

(8	0	2)	4	2	5	—	5	1	5	0
huit	zéro	deux	quatre	deux	cinq		cinq	un	cinq	zéro

(8	0	2)	9	8	5	—	9	5	7	0
huit	zéro	deux	neuf	huit	cinq		neuf	cinq	sept	zéro

Les Couleurs

(lay) *(koo-luhr)*

colors

Les **couleurs** *(koo-luhr)* **sont** *(soh⁽ⁿ⁾)* the same **en** *(ah⁽ⁿ⁾)* **France et** *(frah⁽ⁿ⁾s)* **au** *(oh)* **Québec** *(kay-bek)* as they are in the United States — they just

have different **noms.** *(noh⁽ⁿ⁾)* You can easily recognize **violet** *(vee-oh-lay)* as violet and **bleu** *(bluh)* as blue. Let's learn the

basic **couleurs** *(koo-luhr)* so when you are invited to someone's **maison et** *(may-zoh⁽ⁿ⁾)* you want to bring flowers, you

will be able to order the color you want. Once you've learned **les couleurs,** *(koo-luhr)* quiz yourself. What

color are your shoes? Your eyes? Your hair? Your house?

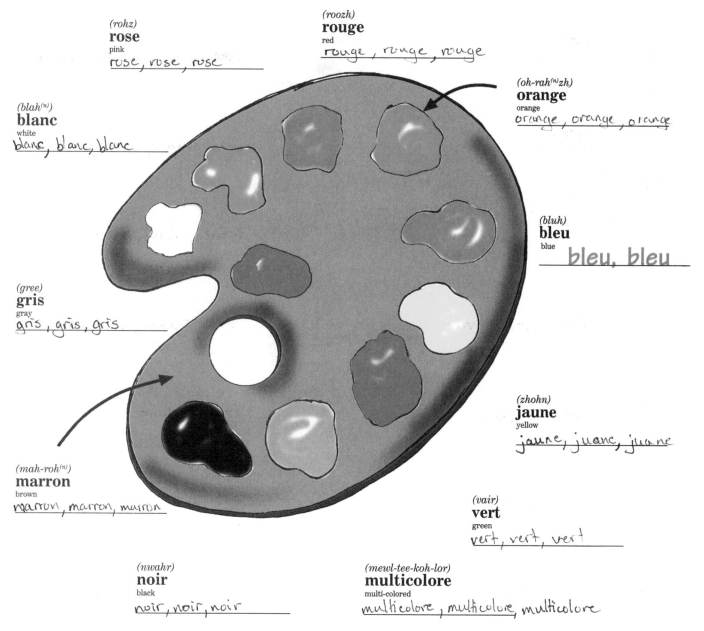

(rohz)
rose
pink
rose, rose, rose

(roozh)
rouge
red
rouge, rouge, rouge

(oh-rah⁽ⁿ⁾zh)
orange
orange
orange, orange, orange

(blah⁽ⁿ⁾)
blanc
white
blanc, blanc, blanc

(bluh)
bleu
blue
bleu, bleu

(gree)
gris
gray
gris, gris, gris

(zhohn)
jaune
yellow
jaune, jaune, jaune

(mah-roh⁽ⁿ⁾)
marron
brown
marron, marron, marron

(vair)
vert
green
vert, vert, vert

(nwahr)
noir
black
noir, noir, noir

(mewl-tee-koh-lor)
multicolore
multi-colored
multicolore, multicolore, multicolore

☑	**la compagnie** (koh⁽ⁿ⁾-pahn-yee)	company	la compagnie, la compagnie, la compagnie
☑	**le/la concierge** (koh⁽ⁿ⁾-see-airzh)	doorkeeper	le/la concierge, le/la concierge, le/la concierge
☑	**la conversation** (koh⁽ⁿ⁾-vair-sah-syoh⁽ⁿ⁾)	conversation	la conversation, la conversation, la conversation
☑	**le cousin** (koo-za⁽ⁿ⁾)	cousin (male)	le cousin, le cousin, le cousin
☑	**la cousine** (koo-zeen)	cousin (female)	la cousine, la cousine, la cousine

c

Peel off the next group of labels **et** proceed to label these **couleurs** *(koo-luhr)* in your **maison.** *(may-zoh⁽ⁿ⁾)* house Identify the

two **ou** *(oo)* or three dominant colors in the flags below.

 Algeria — blanc, vert

 Belgium — noir, juane, rouge

 Cameroon — vert, rouge, juane

 Canada — rouge, blanc

 Chad — bleu ~~bleu~~, juane, rouge

 France — ~~bleu~~ bleu, blanc, rouge

 French Guiana — bleu ~~bleu~~, blanc, rouge

 Haiti — bleu, rouge, blanc, vert

 Ivory Coast — orange, blanc, vert

 Luxembourg — rouge, blanc, bleu

 Madagascar — blanc, rouge, vert

 Mali — vert, juane, rouge

 Monaco — rouge, blanc

 Switzerland — rouge, blanc

You should be able to use your **français** *(frah⁽ⁿ⁾-say)* language skills in any of the above countries as well as in

France.

 Où ___ Où ___ **est le taxi?** *(tahx-ee)*
(where) (where)

 Que ___ Que est-ce ___ **?**
(what) (what is that)

☑	**la dame** *(dahm)*	lady	La dame, la dame, la dame
☑	**la danse** *(dah⁽ⁿ⁾s)*	dance	La danse, la danse, la danse
☑	**décembre** *(day-sah⁽ⁿ⁾m-bruh)*	December	décembre, décembre, décembre
☑	**la déclaration** *(day-klah-rah-syoh⁽ⁿ⁾)*	declaration	la déclaration, la déclaration, le déclar
☑	**le départ** *(day-par)*	departure	le départ, le départ, le départ

d

16

(lahmp)
la **lampe**

(kah-nah-pay)
le **canapé**

(shehz)
la **chaise**

(tah-pee)
le **tapis**

(tah-bluh)
la **table**

(port)
la **porte**

(pah$^{(n)}$-dewl)
la **pendule**

(ree-doh)
le **rideau**

(tay-lay-fohn)
le **téléphone**

(fuh-net-ruh)
la **fenêtre**

(tah-bloh)
le **tableau**

(may-zoh$^{(n)}$)
la **maison**

(bew-roh)
le **bureau**

(sahl) *(ba$^{(n)}$)*
salle de bains

(kwee-zeen)
la **cuisine**

(shah$^{(n)}$-bruh) *(koo-shay)*
chambre à coucher

(sahl) *(mah$^{(n)}$-zhay)*
salle à manger

(lee-veeng-room)
le **living-room**

(gah-rahzh)
le **garage**

(soo-sohl)
le **sous-sol**

(loh-toh)
l'**auto**

(moh-toh)
la **moto**

(vay-loh)
le **vélo**

(shah)
le **chat**

(zhar-da$^{(n)}$)
le **jardin**

(fluhr)
les **fleurs**

(shya$^{(n)}$)
le **chien**

(bwaht) *(oh)* *(let-ruh)*
la **boîte aux lettres**

(koo-ree-ay)
le **courrier**

(zay-roh)
0 **zéro**

(uh$^{(n)}$)
1 **un**

(duh)
2 **deux**

(twah)
3 **trois**

(kah-truh)
4 **quatre**

(sank)
5 **cinq**

(seess)
6 **six**

(set)
7 **sept**

(wheat)
8 **huit**

(nuf)
9 **neuf**

(deess)
10 **dix**

(mah-roh$^{(n)}$)
marron

(roozh)
rouge

(rohz)
rose

(oh-rah$^{(n)}$zh)
orange

(blah$^{(n)}$)
blanc

(zhohn)
jaune

(gree)
gris

(nwahr)
noir

(bluh)
bleu

(vair)
vert

(mewl-tee-koh-lor)
multicolore

(boh$^{(n)}$-zhoor)
bonjour

(boh$^{(n)}$-swahr)
bonsoir

(bun) *(nwee)*
bonne nuit

(sah-lew)
salut

(oh) *(ruh-vwahr)*
au revoir

(koh-mah$^{(n)}$) *(tah-lay-voo)*
Comment allez-vous?

(ray-free-zhay-rah-tuhr)
le **réfrigérateur**

(kwee-zeen-yair)
la **cuisinière**

(va$^{(n)}$)
le **vin**

(bee-air)
la **bière**

(lay)
le **lait**

(buhr)
le **beurre**

(sel)
le **sel**

(pwah-vruh)
le **poivre**

(vair) *(va$^{(n)}$)*
le **verre à vin**

(vair)
le **verre**

(zhoor-nahl)
le **journal**

(tahs)
la **tasse**

(kwee-air)
la **cuillère**

(koo-toh)
le **couteau**

(sair-vyet)
la **serviette**

(lah-syet)
l'**assiette**

(foor-shet)
la **fourchette**

(plah-kar)
le **placard**

(tay)
le **thé**

(kah-fay)
le **café**

(pa$^{(n)}$)
le **pain**

(seel) *(voo)* *(play)*
s'il vous plaît

(mair-see)
merci

STICKY LABELS

This book has over 150 special sticky labels for you to use as you learn new words. When you are introduced to one of these words, remove the corresponding label from these pages. Be sure to use each of these unique self-adhesive labels by adhering them to a picture, window, lamp, or whatever object they refer to. And yes, they are removable! The sticky labels make learning to speak French much more fun and a lot easier than you ever expected. For example, when you look in the mirror and see the label, say

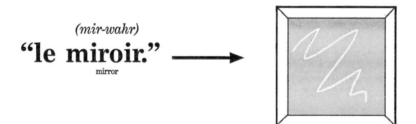

(mir-wahr)
"le miroir."
mirror

Don't just say it once, say it again and again. And once you label the refrigerator, you should never again open that door without saying

(ray-free-zhay-rah-tuhr)
"le réfrigérateur."
refrigerator

By using the sticky labels, you not only learn new words, but friends and family learn along with you! The sooner you start, the sooner you can use these labels at home or work.

7   L'Argent

(lar-zhah⁽ⁿ⁾)

money

Before starting this Step, go back and review Step 5. It is important that you can count to

(va⁽ⁿ⁾)
vingt without looking at **le livre**. Let's learn the larger **nombres** now. After practicing aloud
twenty   *(lee-vruh)*   book   *(nohm-bruh)*

(lay)   *(frah⁽ⁿ⁾-say)*
les nombres français 10 through 1,000 below, write these **nombres** in the blanks provided.

Again, notice the similarities (underlined) between **nombres** such as **quatre** (4), **quatorze** (14),
(kah-truh)   *(kah-torz)*

(kah-rah⁽ⁿ⁾t)
et quarante (40).

10	**dix** *(deess)*	dix, dix, dix, dix, dix, dix, dix, dix, dix, dix, dix, dix, dix, dix, dix, dix
20	**vingt** *(va⁽ⁿ⁾)*	vingt, vingt, vingt, vingt, vingt, vingt, vingt, vingt, vingt
30	**trente** *(trah⁽ⁿ⁾t)*	trente, trente, trente, trente, trente, trente, trente, trente, trente
40	**quarante** *(kah-rah⁽ⁿ⁾t)*	quarante, quarante, quarante, quarante, quarante
50	**cinquante** *(sang-kah⁽ⁿ⁾t)*	cinquante, cinquante, cinquante, cinquante, cinquante
60	**soixante** *(swah-sah⁽ⁿ⁾t)*	soixante, soixante, soixante, soixante, soixante
70	**soixante-dix** (60+10) *(swah-sah⁽ⁿ⁾t-deess)*	soixante-dix, soixante-dix, soixante-dix
80	**quatre-vingts** (4 x 20) *(kah-truh-va⁽ⁿ⁾)*	quatre-vingts, quatre-vingts, quatre-vingts
90	**quatre-vingt-dix** (4 x 20+10) *(kah-truh-va⁽ⁿ⁾-deess)*	quatre-vingts-dix, quatre-vingts-dix
100	**cent** *(sah⁽ⁿ⁾)*	cent, cent, cent, cent, cent, cent, cent, cent, cent, cent
500	**cinq cents** *(sank) (sah⁽ⁿ⁾)*	cinq cents, cinq cents, cinq cents, cinq cents, cinq cents
1,000	**mille** *(meel)*	mille, mille, mille, mille, mille, mille, mille, mille, mille, mille

(duh)
Here are **deux** important phrases to go with all these **nombres**. Say them out loud over and over

and then write them out twice as many times.

(zhay)
j'ai   j'ai, j'ai, j'ai, j'ai, j'ai, j'ai, j'ai, j'ai, j'ai, j'ai
I have

(noo)   *(zah-voh⁽ⁿ⁾)*
nous avons   nous avons, nous avons, nous avons, nous avons, nous avons
we   have

☑	**déjà** *(day-zhah)*	already	déjà, déjà, déjà
	– **déjà vu** *(day-zhah)(vew)* ...	already seen	-déjà vu, -déjà vu, -déjà vu
☑	**la désir** *(day-zeer)*	desire	la desire, la desire, la desire
☑	**la distance** *(dee-stah⁽ⁿ⁾s)*	distance	la distance, la distance, la distance
☑	**le docteur** *(dohk-tur)*	doctor	le docteur, le docteur, le docteur

d

The unit of currency **en France** *(ay)* **est l'euro**, *(luh-roh)* abbreviated "€". Let's learn the various kinds of
in *is*

(moh-nay) *(bee-ay)* *(moh)*
monnaie et billets. Always be sure to practice each **mot** out loud. You might want to exchange
coins *bills*

(ma⁽ⁿ⁾-tuh-nah⁽ⁿ⁾) *(ah-vek)* *(ar-zhah⁽ⁿ⁾)*
some money **maintenant** so that you can familiarize yourself **avec** the various types of **argent**.
now *with* *money*

Billets *(bee-ay)*
bills

Monnaie *(moh-nay)*
coins

(sank) (uh-roh)
cinq euros

(sah⁽ⁿ⁾-teem)
deux centimes

cinq centimes

(deess)
dix euros

dix centimes

(vah⁽ⁿ⁾)
vingt euros

vingt centimes

cinquante centimes

(sang-kah⁽ⁿ⁾t)
cinquante euros
50

(uh-roh)
un euro

deux euros

---

l'économie, l'économie, l'économie
l'entrée, l'entrée, l'entrée
est, est, est
l'état, l'état, l'état
—Les États-Unis, —Les États-Unis,
—Les États-Unis

Review **les nombres dix** *(deess)* through **mille** *(meel)* again. **Maintenant,** *(ma(n)-tuh-nah(n))* / now how do you say "twenty-two" **ou** *(oo)* "fifty-three" **en français?** *(ah(n))* Put the numbers together in a logical sequence just as you do in English. See if you can say **et** write out **les nombres** on this **page**. *(pahzh)* / page The answers **sont** *(soh(n))* / are at the bottom of **la page**.

1. _____ vingt-cinq _____
$(25 = 20 + 5)$

2. _____ quatre-~~vingt~~ vingts - trois _____
$(83 = 80 + 3)$

3. _____ qaurante -sept _____
$(47 = 40 + 7)$

4. _____ quatre-vingt-seize _____
$(96 = 90 + 6)$

Now, how would you say the following **en français?** *(frah(n)-say)*

5. _____ J'ai quatre-vingts euros. _____
(I have 80 euros.)

6. _____ Nous avons soixante-douze euros. _____
(We have 72 euros.)

To ask how much something costs **en français,** one asks — **Combien** *(kohm-bya(n))* **ça** *(sah)* **coûte?** *(koot)*

Now you try it. _____ Combien ça coûte? _____
(How much does that cost?)

Answer the following questions based on the numbers in parentheses.

7. **Combien** *(kohm-bya(n))* **ça** *(sah)* **coûte?** *(koot)* / that costs **Ça coûte** _____ dix _____ **euros.**
that costs (10)

8. **Combien coûte** *(koot)* **le ticket?** *(tee-kay)* **Le ticket coûte** _____ vingt _____ **euros.**
costs (20)

9. **Combien coûte le livre?** *(lee-vruh)* / book **Le livre coûte** _____ dix-sept _____ **euros.**
(17)

10. **Combien coûte le film?** *(feelm)* **Le film coûte** _____ cinq _____ **euros.**
(5)

(oh-zhoor-dwee) (duh-ma(n)) (ee-air)
Aujourd'hui, Demain et Hier
today   tomorrow   and   yesterday

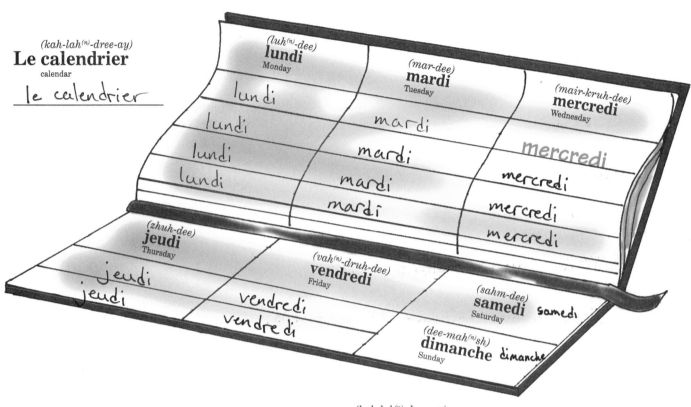

(kah-lah(n)-dree-ay)
Le calendrier
calendar

le calendrier

Learn the days of the week by writing them in **le calendrier** *(kah-lah(n)-dree-ay)* above **et** then move on to the

(kah-truh)   *(zhoor)*
quatre parts to each **jour.**
four   day

(mah-ta(n))
le matin
morning

le matin

(lah-preh-mee-dee)
l'après-midi
afternoon

l'après-midi

(swahr)
le soir
evening

le soir

(nwee)
la nuit
night

la nuit

☑ **la fatigue** *(fah-teeg)*	fatigue, tiredness		la fatigue, la fatigue la fatigue
– **je suis fatigué** *(zhuh)(swee)(fah-tee-gay)* . .	I am tired		je suis fatigué, je suis fatigué, je suis fatigué
☐ **la fête** *(fet)*	feast, festival	**f**	
☐ **le festival** *(feh-stee-vahl)*	festival		
☐ **le film** *(feelm)*	film		

Il *(eel)* **est** *(ay)* **très** *(treh)* **important** *(za(n)-por-tah(n))* to know the days of the week **et** the various parts of the day as well as
very   important

these **trois mots.**

(ee-air) **hier**   *(oh-zhoor-dwee)* **aujourd'hui**   *(duh-ma(n))* **demain**

(dee-mah(n)sh) **dimanche**
Sunday

(luh(n)-dee) **lundi**
Monday

(mar-dee) **mardi**
Tuesday

(mair-kruh-dee) **mercredi**
Wednesday

(zhuh-dee) **jeudi**
Thursday

(vah(n)-druh-dee) **vendredi**
Friday

(sahm-dee) **samedi**
Saturday

Quel *(kel)* **jour** *(zhoor)* **sommes-nous aujourd'hui?** *(sohm-noo)* _____
what   day   are   we

Quel jour étions-nous hier? *(ay-tee-oh(n)-noo)* _____
were   we

_____ **nous serons** *(noo)* *(sair-oh(n))* **mercredi et** _____
(tomorrow)   will be

Quel jour serons-nous demain? *(kel)* *(sair-oh(n)-noo)* _____
will we be

Aujourd'hui nous sommes mardi, non? *(noo)* *(sohm)* So,
are

nous étions *(noo)* *(zay-tee-oh(n))* **lundi.** Starting from
(yesterday)   were

aujourd'hui, Monday **c'est "lundi."**

a.	Sunday morning	=	_____
b.	Friday morning	=	_____
c.	Saturday evening	=	_____
d.	Thursday afternoon	=	*jeudi après-midi*
e.	Thursday night	=	_____
f.	yesterday evening	=	_____
g.	tomorrow afternoon	=	_____
h.	tomorrow evening	=	_____

_____ **est le concert?** *(ay)* *(koh(n)-sair)*
(when)   (when)   concert

_____ **est-ce?** *(ess)*
(who)   (who)   is it

RÉPONSES

				f.	hier soir
			e.	jeudi nuit	c.	samedi soir
h.	demain soir				b.	vendredi matin
g.	demain après-midi	d.	jeudi après-midi		a.	dimanche matin

RÉPONSES

a. dimanche matin
b. vendredi matin
c. samedi soir
d. jeudi après-midi
e. jeudi nuit
f. hier soir
g. demain après-midi
h. demain soir

Knowing the parts of **le jour** will help you to learn the various **salutations** *(sah-lew-tah-syoh⁽ⁿ⁾)* **françaises** *(frah⁽ⁿ⁾-sez)* below.
day · greetings

Practice these every day until your trip.

(boh⁽ⁿ⁾-zhoor)
bonjour _____
good morning/good day

(boh⁽ⁿ⁾-swahr)
bonsoir _____
good evening

(bun) *(nwee)*
bonne nuit _____
good · night

(sah-lew)
salut _____
hello/hi

(oh) *(ruh-vwahr)*
au revoir _____
goodbye

Take the next **quatre** labels **et** stick them on the appropriate **choses** *(shohz)* in your **maison** *(may-zoh⁽ⁿ⁾)*. Make sure
four · things · house

you attach them to the correct items, as they are only **en français** *(ah⁽ⁿ⁾)*. How about the bathroom

mirror **pour** *(poor)* "**bonjour**"? **Ou** *(oo)* your alarm clock for "**bonne nuit** *(bun) (nwee)*"? Let's not forget,
for · or

(koh-mah⁽ⁿ⁾) *(tah-lay-voo)*
Comment allez-vous? _____
how are you

Now for some "**oui**" *(wee)* or "**non**" *(noh⁽ⁿ⁾)* questions –
yes · no

Are your eyes **bleus**? *(bluh)* _____   Are your shoes **marron**? *(mah-roh⁽ⁿ⁾)* _____

Is your favorite color **rouge**? *(roozh)* _____   Is today **samedi**? _____

Do you own a **chien**? *(shya⁽ⁿ⁾)* _____   Do you own a **chat**? *(shah)* _____

You **êtes** *(et)* about one-fourth of your way through this **livre** *(lee-vruh)* **et** **c'est** *(say)* a good time to quickly review
are · book · it is

les mots you have learned before doing the crossword puzzle on the next **page**. **Amusez-vous** *(ah-mew-zay-voo)*
enjoy yourself

et bonne chance! *(bun) (shah⁽ⁿ⁾s)*
good · luck

RÉPONSES TO THE CROSSWORD PUZZLE (MOTS CROISÉS)

ACROSS

1. je voudrais
2. avec
3. avons
4. Amérique
5. monnaie
6. ticket d'autobus
7. samedi
8. banque
9. dix-neuf
10. nuit
11. thé
12. vingt
13. mercredi
14. chaise
15. homme
16. cinquante
17. pendule
18. aujourd'hui
20. eau
21. cinq
22. quatre
23. et
24. voilà
25. comment
26. jaune
27. multicolore
28. trois
29. tableau
30. rideau

DOWN

1. jours
2. carte postale
3. noir
4. l'après-midi
5. auto
6. réponse
7. salut
8. qui
9. qu'est-ce que c'est
10. argent
11. femme
12. un
13. mardi
14. nous avons
15. blanc
16. pourquoi
17. pièce
18. lampe
20. rouge
21. vert
22. vendredi
23. maison
25. gris
26. combien
27. quand
28. deux

24

CROSSWORD PUZZLE (MOTS CROISÉS) *(kwah-zay)*

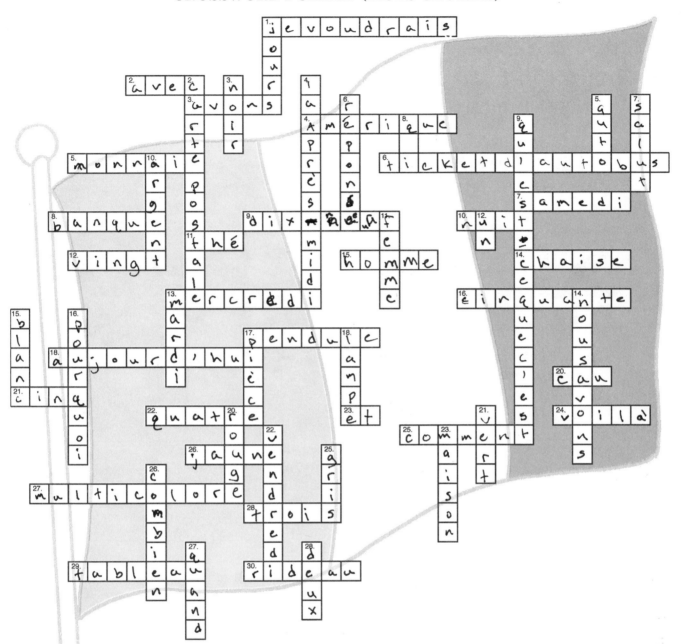

ACROSS

1. I would like
2. with
3. (we) have
4. America
5. coins
6. bus ticket
7. Saturday
8. bank
9. 19
10. night
11. tea
12. 20
13. Wednesday
14. chair
15. man
16. 50
17. clock
18. today
20. water
21. five
22. four
23. and
24. there is
25. how?
26. yellow
27. multi-colored
28. three
29. picture
30. curtain

DOWN

1. days
2. postcard
3. black
4. the afternoon
5. car
6. response, answer
7. hi
8. who?
9. what is it?
10. money
11. woman
12. a (masculine)
13. Tuesday
14. we have
15. white
16. why?
17. room
18. lamp
20. red
21. green
22. Friday
23. house
25. gray
26. how much?
27. when?
28. two

☐ **le filtre** *(feel-truh)* . . . . filter
 – **un café filtre** *(kah-fay) (feel-truh)* . . . . filtered coffee **f** _____
☐ **la fin** *(fa⁽ⁿ⁾)* . . . . end _____
☐ **le fonctionnaire** *(foh⁽ⁿ⁾-syoh-nair)* . . . . functionary, civil servant _____
☐ **le football** *(foot-bahl)* . . . . soccer _____

9 Dans, sur, sous...

(dah⁽ⁿ⁾) in   *(sewr)* on   *(soo)* under

Les prépositions *(pray-poh-zee-syoh⁽ⁿ⁾)* **françaises** *(frah⁽ⁿ⁾-sez)* (words like "in," "on," "through" and "next to") **sont** easy to
are

learn, **et** they allow you to be precise **avec** a minimum of effort. Instead of having to point **six** *(seess)*

times at a piece of yummy pastry you would like, you can explain precisely which one you want

by saying **il est** behind, in front of, next to **ou** under the piece of pastry that the salesperson is
(eel) *it is*

starting to pick up. Let's learn some of these **petits mots.** *(puh-tee)* *little*

(soo)
sous _____
under

(dah⁽ⁿ⁾)
dans _____
into/in

(oh-duh-syoo) *(duh)*
au-dessus de* _____
over

(duh-vah⁽ⁿ⁾)
devant _____
in front of

(ah⁽ⁿ⁾-truh)
entre _____ entre, entre, entre _____
between

(dair-ee-air)
derrière _____
behind

(ah) (koh-tay) (duh)
à côté de* _____
next to

(duh)
de* _____
out of/from

(sewr)
sur _____
on

(pah-tee-suh-ree)
la pâtisserie _____
pastry!

*****Note that "de" sometimes combines with "la," "le" or "les" to form "de la," "du," *(de+le)* "de l'" and

(de+les)
"des." Fill in the blanks on the next **page** with the correct prepositions.

_____ allez-vous?
(how) *(how)* *are you*

_____ le taxi est-il jaune?
(why) *(why)* *(ay-teel)* *(zhohn)* *yellow*

- ☐ **la forme** *(form)* . . . . form, shape
- ☐ **la forêt** *(foh-ray)* . . . . forest
- ☐ **le foyer** *(fwah-yay)* . . . . home, hearth
- ☐ **franc/franche** *(frah⁽ⁿ⁾)/(frah⁽ⁿ⁾sh)* . . . . frank, honest
- ☐ **le fruit** *(fwee)* . . . . fruit

f _____
_____
_____
_____
_____

26

(pah-tee-suh-ree)
La pâtisserie est _____ **la table.**
pastry   (on)   table
(tah-bluh)

(shya⁽ⁿ⁾)
Le chien est _____ **la table.**
dog   (under)   table
(tah-bluh)

(dohk-tur)
Le docteur est _____ **le bon hôtel.**
doctor   (in)   good
(boh⁽ⁿ⁾) (oh-tel)

(oo) (ay)
Où est le docteur? _____

(lohm)
L'homme est _____ **l'hôtel.**
man   (in front of)

Où est l'homme? _____

(tay-lay-fohn)
Le téléphone est _____ **tableau.**
telephone   (next to the)   picture
(tah-bloh)

Où est le téléphone? _____

(ma⁽ⁿ⁾-tuh-nah⁽ⁿ⁾)
Maintenant, fill in each blank on the picture below with the best possible one of these **petits**
now   little
(puh-tee)

mots. Do you recognize **la Cathédrale Notre-Dame** below?
           (kah-tay-drahl) (noh-truh-dahm)

_____ (over)

_____ (between)

_____ (next to)

_____ (behind)

_____ (in, into)

_____ (under)

_____ (in front of)

❑ **la galerie** *(gah-leh-ree)*	gallery, long room	_____
❑ **la géographie** *(zhay-oh-grah-fee)*	geography	_____
❑ **la glace** *(glahs)*	ice cream **g**	_____
❑ **la gomme** *(gohm)*	eraser	_____
❑ **le gourmand** *(goor-mah⁽ⁿ⁾)*	gourmand, glutton	_____

27

You have learned the days of **la** *(suh-men)* **semaine,** so now *(say)* **c'est le** *(moh-mah⁽ⁿ⁾)* **moment** to learn **les** *(mwah)* **mois** *(duh)* **de** *(lah-nay)* **l'année** **et** all the different kinds of *(tah⁽ⁿ⁾)* **temps.**

week   it is   months   of   the year

weather

(zhah⁽ⁿ⁾-vee-ay) **janvier**	*(fay-vree-ay)* **février**	*(marss)* **mars**	*(ah-vreel)* **avril**
		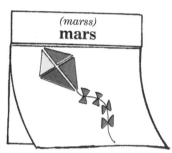	
(may) **mai**	*(zhwa⁽ⁿ⁾)* **juin**	*(zhwee-ay)* **juillet**	*(oot)* **août**

(sep-tah⁽ⁿ⁾m-bruh) **septembre**	*(ohk-toh-bruh)* **octobre**	*(noh-vah⁽ⁿ⁾m-bruh)* **novembre**	*(day-sah⁽ⁿ⁾m-bruh)* **décembre**

When someone asks, "**Quel temps fait-il aujourd'hui?**" you have a variety of answers. Let's

(kel) *(tah⁽ⁿ⁾)* *(fay-teel)* *(oh-zhoor-dwee)*

what   (the) weather does it make   today

learn them but first, does this sound familiar?

Trente jours *(oh⁽ⁿ⁾)* **ont** *(sep-tah⁽ⁿ⁾m-bruh)* **septembre,** *(ah-vreel)* **avril,** *(zhwa⁽ⁿ⁾)* **juin** **et** *(noh-vah⁽ⁿ⁾m-bruh)* **novembre...**

have

☐	**le gourmet** *(goor-may)*	gourmet, epicurean	_____
☐	**le gouvernement** *(goo-vair-nuh-mah⁽ⁿ⁾)*	government	_____
☐	**grand** *(grah⁽ⁿ⁾)*	big	**g** _____
☐	**la grandeur** *(grah⁽ⁿ⁾-dur)*	greatness	_____
☐	**le guide** *(geed)*	guide	_____

(kel)   *(tah^(n))*   *(fay-teel)*   *(oh-zhoor-dwee)*
Quel temps fait-il aujourd'hui? _____
what   today

(nehzh) *(ah^(n))*
Il neige en janvier. _____
it   snows   in

(oh-see)
Il neige aussi en février. _____
aussi
also

(pluh)
Il pleut en mars. _____
it   rains

(oh-see)
Il pleut aussi en avril. _____

(fay) *(dew)* *(vah^(n))*
Il fait du vent en mai. _____
makes   windy

(soh-lay)
Il fait du soleil en juin. _____
sunny

(boh)
Il fait beau en juillet. _____
beautiful

(shoh)
Il fait chaud en août. _____
hot

(broo-ee-yar)
Il fait du brouillard en septembre. _____
foggy

(fay) *(fray)*
Il fait frais en octobre. _____
cool

(moh-vay)
Il fait mauvais en novembre. _____
bad

(fwah)
Il fait froid en décembre. _____
cold

(kel)   *(ah^(n))*
Quel temps fait-il en février? _____
in

Quel temps fait-il en avril? _____ Il pleut en avril. Il pleut en avril. _____

Quel temps fait-il en mai? _____

Quel temps fait-il en août? _____

Maintenant, les saisons de l'année...
(say-zoh⁽ⁿ⁾)
seasons of the year

(lee-vair)
l'hiver
winter

(lay-tay)
l'été
summer

(loh-tohn)
l'automne
autumn

(prah⁽ⁿ⁾-tah⁽ⁿ⁾)
le printemps
spring

(sel-see-ews)
Celsius
Centigrade

Fahrenheit
Fahrenheit

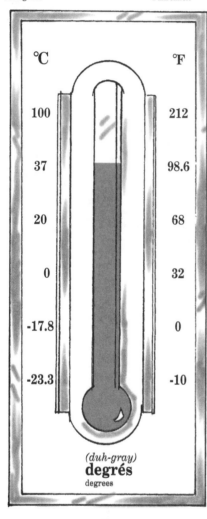

°C	°F
100	212
37	98.6
20	68
0	32
-17.8	0
-23.3	-10

(duh-gray)
degrés
degrees

At this point, **c'est une bonne idée** to familiarize *(say) (tewn) (bun) (ee-day)* good

yourself **avec les températures européennes.** *(tah⁽ⁿ⁾-pay-rah-tewr) (uh-roh-pay-yen)* temperatures European

Carefully study **le thermomètre** because **les** *(tair-moh-meh-truh)*

températures en Europe are calculated on the *(tah⁽ⁿ⁾-pay-rah-tewr) (uh-rohp)*

basis of Centigrade (not Fahrenheit).

To convert °F to °C, subtract 32 and multiply by 0.55.

98.6 °F - 32 = 66.6 x 0.55 = 37 °C

To convert °C to °F, multiply by 1.8 and add 32.

37 °C x 1.8 = 66.6 + 32 = 98.6 °F

What is normal body temperature in **Celsius?**

What is the freezing point in **Celsius?**

Foyer, Faim et Foi!
(fwah-yay) home *(fa⁽ⁿ⁾)* hunger *(fwah)* faith

Just as we have the three "R's" **en anglais, en français** there are the three "F's" which help us

to understand some of the basics of **la vie française et la famille française**. Study the family

(vee) life *(frah⁽ⁿ⁾-sez)* French *(fah-mee-yuh)* family

tree below.

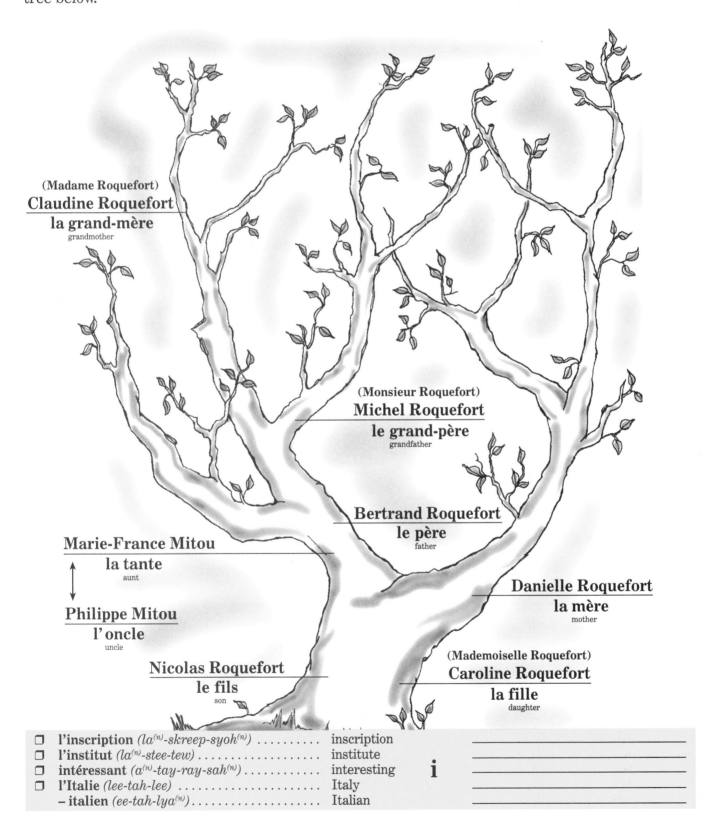

(Madame Roquefort)
Claudine Roquefort
la grand-mère
grandmother

(Monsieur Roquefort)
Michel Roquefort
le grand-père
grandfather

Bertrand Roquefort
le père
father

Marie-France Mitou
la tante
aunt

↕

Philippe Mitou
l' oncle
uncle

Danielle Roquefort
la mère
mother

Nicolas Roquefort
le fils
son

(Mademoiselle Roquefort)
Caroline Roquefort
la fille
daughter

☐ **l'inscription** *(la⁽ⁿ⁾-skreep-syoh⁽ⁿ⁾)* . . . . inscription
☐ **l'institut** *(la⁽ⁿ⁾-stee-tew)* . . . . institute
☐ **intéressant** *(a⁽ⁿ⁾-tay-ray-sah⁽ⁿ⁾)* . . . . interesting
☐ **l'Italie** *(lee-tah-lee)* . . . . Italy
☐ **– italien** *(ee-tah-lya⁽ⁿ⁾)* . . . . Italian

i

_____
_____
_____
_____
_____

Let's learn how to identify **la famille** *(fah-mee-yuh)* by **nom.** *(noh⁽ⁿ⁾)* Study the following **exemples** *(eg-zah⁽ⁿ⁾-pluh)* carefully.
family / name / examples

Comment vous appelez-vous? *(voo)* *(zah-puh-lay-voo)* _____
what is your name/how are you called

Je m'appelle *(mah-pel)* _____.
my name is/I am called   (your name)

les parents *(pah-rah⁽ⁿ⁾)*
parents

le père *(pair)* _____
father

Comment s'appelle le père? *(koh-moh⁽ⁿ⁾)* *(sah-pel)* _____
how / is called / father

la mère *(mair)* _____
mother

Comment s'appelle la mère? _____
how / mother

les enfants *(lay) (zah⁽ⁿ⁾-fah⁽ⁿ⁾)*   **Le fils et la fille** *(feess) (fee-yuh)* **sont aussi frère** *(frair)* **et soeur.** *(suhr)*
children / brother / sister

le fils *(feess)* _____
son

Comment s'appelle le fils? *(feess)* _____
son

la fille *(fee-yuh)* _____
daughter

Comment s'appelle la fille? *(fee-yuh)* _____
daughter

les parents *(pah-rah⁽ⁿ⁾)*
relatives

le grand-père *(grah⁽ⁿ⁾-pair)* _____
grandfather

Comment s'appelle le grand-père? *(koh-mah⁽ⁿ⁾)* *(sah-pel)* _____
grandfather

la grand-mère *(grah⁽ⁿ⁾-mair)* _____
grandmother

Comment s'appelle la grand-mère? _____
grandmother

Now you ask —

_____
(How are you called?/What is your name?)

And answer —

_____
(My name is . . .)

❒	**la jaquette** *(zhah-ket)*	woman's jacket	_____
❒	**le Japon** *(zhah-poh⁽ⁿ⁾)*	Japan	_____
	– **japonais** *(zhah-poh-nay)*	Japanese **j**	_____
❒	**le journal** *(zhoor-nahl)*	newspaper	_____
❒	**La Joconde** *(zhoh-kohnd)*	Mona Lisa (in the Louvre)	

(kwee-zeen)
La Cuisine
kitchen

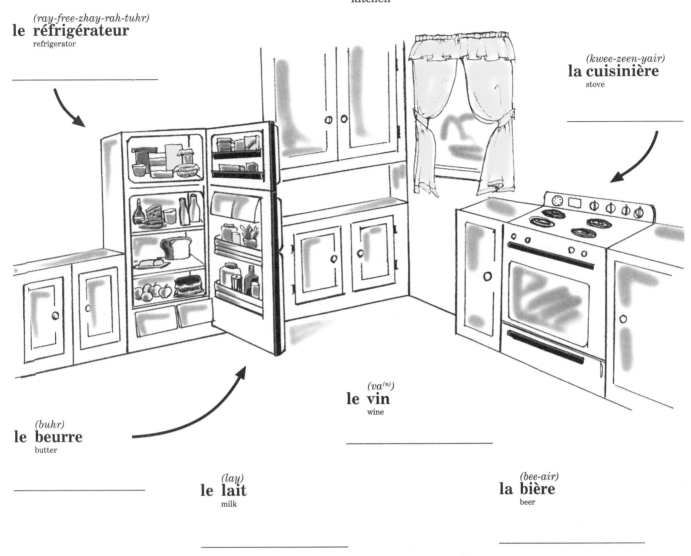

(ray-free-zhay-rah-tuhr)
le réfrigérateur
refrigerator

_____

(kwee-zeen-yair)
la cuisinière
stove

_____

(buhr)
le beurre
butter

_____

(va⁽ⁿ⁾)
le vin
wine

_____

(lay)
le lait
milk

_____

(bee-air)
la bière
beer

_____

Answer these questions aloud.

(bee-air)
Où est la bière? . . . . **La bière est dans le réfrigérateur.** *(ray-free-zhay-rah-tuhr)*
beer

(luh)
Où est le lait?
milk

(va⁽ⁿ⁾)
Où est le vin?
wine

(buhr)
Où est le beurre?
butter

(oo-vray)
Maintenant ouvrez your **livre** to the **page avec** the labels **et** remove the next group of labels **et**
open   book

(shohz)   *(kwee-zeen)*
proceed to label all these **choses** in your **cuisine.**
things   kitchen

❏	**juste** *(zhoost)*	fair, just	
❏	**la justice** *(zhoo-stees)*	justice	**j** _____
❏	**le kilo** *(kee-loh)*	kilogram	_____
❏	**le kilomètre** *(kee-loh-meh-truh)*	kilometer	**k** _____
❏	**le kiosque** *(kee-ohsk)*	kiosk	_____

33

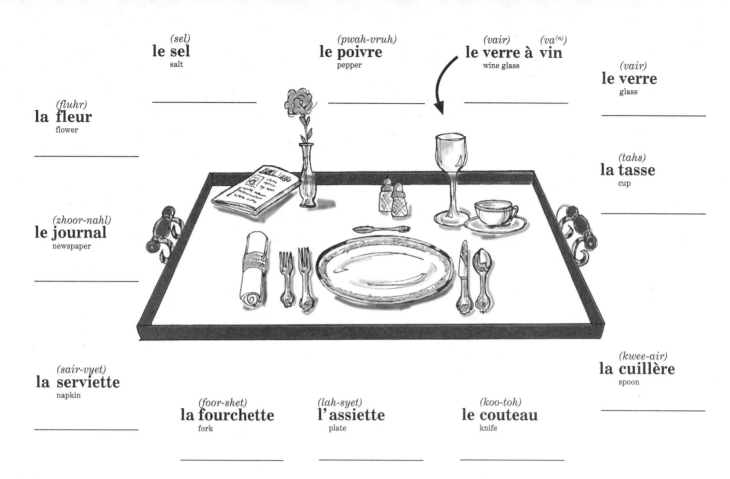

(sel)
le sel
salt

(pwah-vruh)
le poivre
pepper

(vair) *(va$^{(n)}$)*
le verre à vin
wine glass

(vair)
le verre
glass

(fluhr)
la fleur
flower

(tahs)
la tasse
cup

(zhoor-nahl)
le journal
newspaper

(sair-vyet)
la serviette
napkin

(kwee-air)
la cuillère
spoon

(foor-shet)
la fourchette
fork

(lah-syet)
l'assiette
plate

(koo-toh)
le couteau
knife

Et more . . .

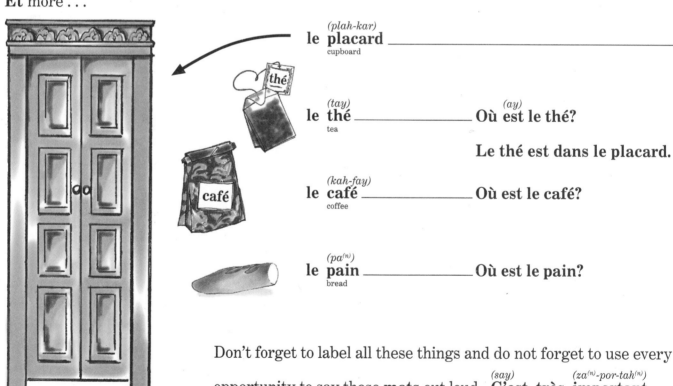

(plah-kar)
le placard
cupboard

(tay)
le thé
tea

(ay)
Où est le thé?

Le thé est dans le placard.

(kah-fay)
le café
coffee

Où est le café?

(pa$^{(n)}$)
le pain
bread

Où est le pain?

Don't forget to label all these things and do not forget to use every

opportunity to say these **mots** out loud. **C'est très important.**
(say) *(za$^{(n)}$-por-tah$^{(n)}$)*
very

1

(par-doh(n)) **pardon**	*(let-ruh)* **la lettre**	*(day-oh-doh-rah(n))* **le déodorant**	*(short)* **le short**
(lar-mwahr) **l'armoire**	*(ta(n)-bruh)* **le timbre**	*(pen-yuh)* **le peigne**	*(tee-shirt)* **le teeshirt**
(lee) **le lit**	*(kart) (poh-stahl)* **la carte postale**	*(mah(n)-toh)* **le manteau**	*(sleep)* **le slip**
(loh-ray-yay) **l'oreiller**	*(pahs-por)* **le passeport**	*(pah-rah-plew-ee)* **le parapluie**	*(my-oh) (kor)* **le maillot de corps**
(koo-vair-teur) **la couverture**	*(bee-yay)* **le billet**	*(la(n)-pair-may-ah-bluh)* **l'imperméable**	*(rohb)* **la robe**
(ray-vay) **le réveil**	*(vah-leez)* **la valise**	*(gah(n))* **les gants**	*(shuh-me-zee-air)* **le chemisier**
(mir-wahr) **le miroir**	*(sahk) (ma(n))* **le sac à main**	*(shah-poh)* **le chapeau**	*(zhewp)* **la jupe**
(lah-vah-boh) **le lavabo**	*(port-fuh-yuh)* **le portefeuille**	*(boht)* **les bottes**	*(pul)* **le pull**
(sair-vyet) **le serviette**	*(lar-zhah(n))* **l'argent**	*(shoh-suhr)* **les chaussures**	*(koh(n)-bee-nay-zoh(n))* **la combinaison**
(doo-bul-vay-say) **le W.C.**	*(kart) (kray-dee)* **les cartes de crédit**	*(teh-nees)* **les tennis**	*(soo-tya(n)-gorzh)* **le soutien-gorge**
(doosh) **la douche**	*(shek) (vwah-yahzh)* **les chèques de voyage**	*(koh(n)-play)* **le complet**	*(sleep)* **le slip**
(kray-yoh(n)) **le crayon**	*(lah-pah-ray-foh-toh)* **l'appareil-photo**	*(krah-vaht)* **la cravate**	*(shoh-set)* **les chaussettes**
(tay-lay-vee-syoh(n)) **la télévision**	*(peh-lee-kewl)* **la pellicule**	*(shuh-meez)* **la chemise**	*(bah)* **les bas**
(stee-loh) **le stylo**	*(my-oh) (ba(n))* **le maillot de bain**	*(moo-shwahr)* **le mouchoir**	*(pee-zhah-mah)* **le pyjama**
(lee-vruh) **le livre**	*(sah(n)-dahl)* **les sandales**	*(veh-stoh(n))* **le veston**	*(shuh-meez) (nwee)* **la chemise de nuit**
(lor-dee-nah-tur) **l'ordinateur**	*(lew-net) (soh-lay)* **les lunettes de soleil**	*(pah(n)-tah-loh(n))* **le pantalon**	*(rohb) (shah(n)-bruh)* **la robe de chambre**
(lew-net) **les lunettes**	*(brohs) (dah(n))* **la brosse à dents**	*(jean)* **le jean**	*(pah(n)-too-fluh)* **les pantoufles**
(pah-pee-ay) **le papier**	*(dah(n)-tee-frees)* **le dentifrice**	*(zhuh) (vya(n)) (duh)* **Je viens de** _____.	
(kor-bay) (pah-pee-ay) **corbeille à papier**	*(sah-voh(n))* **le savon**	*(zhuh) (voo-dray) (zah-prah(n)-druh) (luh) (frah(n)-say)* **Je voudrais apprendre le français.**	
(ruh-vew) **la revue**	*(rah-zwahr)* **le rasoir**	*(zhuh) (mah-pel)* **Je m'appelle** _____.	

PLUS...

This book includes a number of other innovative features unique to the *"10 minutes a day®"* series. At the back of this book, you will find twelve pages of flash cards. Cut them out and flip through them at least once a day.

On pages 116, 117 and 118 you will find a beverage guide and a menu guide. Don't wait until your trip to use them. Clip out the menu guide and use it tonight at the dinner table. Take them both with you the next time you dine at your favorite French restaurant.

By using the special features in this book, you will be speaking French before you know it.

(ah-mew-zay-voo)   *(bun)*   *(shah⁽ⁿ⁾s)*

Amusez-vous et bonne chance!

enjoy yourself   good   luck

(ruh-lee-zhoh⁽ⁿ⁾)

La Religion
religion

En France, there is not the wide variety of *(ruh-lee-zhoh⁽ⁿ⁾)* **religions** that **nous avons** **ici** **en Amérique.**
religions   *(noo)* **nous** *(zah-voh⁽ⁿ⁾)* *(ee-see)* here *(ah-may-reek)*

A person is usually one of the following.

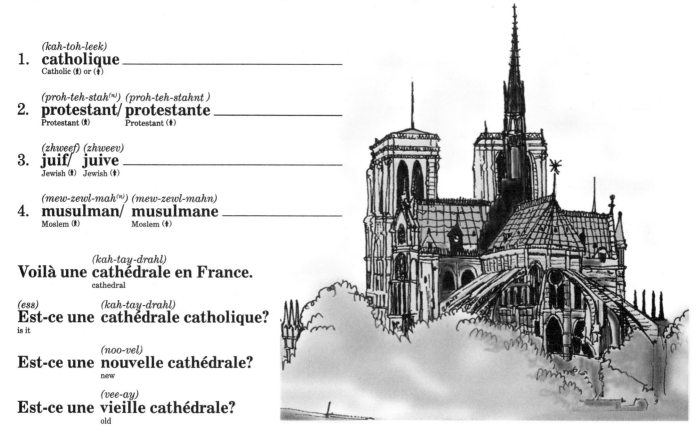

1. *(kah-toh-leek)* **catholique** _____
Catholic (♂) or (♀)

2. *(proh-teh-stah⁽ⁿ⁾)* *(proh-teh-stahnt)* **protestant/ protestante** _____
Protestant (♂)   Protestant (♀)

3. *(zhweef)* *(zhweev)* **juif/ juive** _____
Jewish (♂)   Jewish (♀)

4. *(mew-zewl-mah⁽ⁿ⁾)* *(mew-zewl-mahn)* **musulman/ musulmane** _____
Moslem (♂)   Moslem (♀)

(kah-tay-drahl)
Voilà une cathédrale en France.
cathedral

(ess) *(kah-tay-drahl)*
Est-ce une cathédrale catholique?
is it

(noo-vel)
Est-ce une nouvelle cathédrale?
new

(vee-ay)
Est-ce une vieille cathédrale?
old

Maintenant, let's learn how to say "I am" **en français:** *(zhuh) (swee)* **je suis** _____
now   I   am

Test yourself – write each sentence on the next page for more practice. Add your own personal

variations as well.

Note that to make an adjective feminine **en français,** all you *generally* need to do is add an "e."

This will sometimes vary the pronunciation slightly.

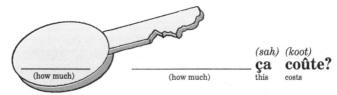

_____   _____ *(sah) (koot)* **ça coûte?**
(how much)   (how much)   this   costs

☐ **le lieu** *(lyuh)* . . . . place _____
☐ **la ligne** *(leen-yuh)* . . . . line _____
☐ **la limonade** *(lee-moh-nahd)* . . . . lemonade _____
☐ **le logement** *(lohzh-mah⁽ⁿ⁾)* . . . . lodging, accommodation _____
☐ **Londres** *(loh⁽ⁿ⁾-druh)* . . . . London

1

Je suis catholique. *(kah-toh-leek)* _____
I am Catholic (♀/♂)

Je suis protestant. *(proh-teh-stah⁽ⁿ⁾)* _____
(♂)

Je suis juif. *(swee) (zhweef)* _____
Jewish (♂)

Je suis américain. *(zhuh) (ah-may-ree-ka⁽ⁿ⁾)* _____
American (♂)

Je suis en Europe. *(uh-rohp)* _____

Je suis canadienne. *(kah-nah-dyen)* _____
Canadian (♀)

Je suis dans l'église. *(dah⁽ⁿ⁾) (lay-gleez)* _____
I am in church

Je suis en France. *(frah⁽ⁿ⁾s)* _____

Je suis musulman. *(mew-zewl-mah⁽ⁿ⁾)* _____
Moslem (♂)

Je suis dans le restaurant. *(reh-stoh-rah⁽ⁿ⁾)* _____

Je suis américaine. *(ah-may-ree-ken)* _____
(♀)

Je suis dans l'hôtel. *(loh-tel)* _____

Je suis dans la maison. _____
I am

Je suis fatigué. *(fah-tee-gay)* _____
I am fatigued/tired

To negate any of these statements, simply add **"ne"** *(nuh)* before the verb and **"pas"** *(pah)* after the verb.
not/no

Je ne suis pas musulman. *(nuh)(swee) (pah) (mew-zewl-mah⁽ⁿ⁾)* _____
I am not

Je ne suis pas français. *(pah)* _____
I am not

Go through and drill these sentences again but with **"ne"** plus **"pas."**

Maintenant, take a piece of paper. Our **famille** *(fah-mee-yuh)* from earlier had a reunion. Identify everyone below by writing **le mot correct en français** for each person — **la mère,** *(mair)* **l'oncle** *(loh⁽ⁿ⁾-kluh)* and so on. Don't forget **le chien!** *(shya⁽ⁿ⁾)*

❏ **le magasin** *(mah-gah-za⁽ⁿ⁾)*	. . . .	store	_____
❏ **le magazine** *(mah-gah-zeen)*	. . . .	magazine	_____
❏ **magnifique** *(mah-nee-feek)*	. . . .	magnificent **m**	_____
❏ **le marchand** *(mar-shah⁽ⁿ⁾)*	. . . .	merchant	_____
❏ **le mécanicien** *(may-kah-nee-sya⁽ⁿ⁾)*	. . . .	mechanic	_____

You have already used *(duh)* **deux** very important verbs: **je** *(voo-dray)* **voudrais** and *(zhay)* **j'ai**. Although you might

I   would like   I   have

be able to get by with only these verbs, let's assume you want to do better. First a quick review.

How do you say   **"I"**   **en** *(frah⁽ⁿ⁾-say)* **français?** _____

How do you say   **"we"**   **en français?** _____

Compare these *(duh)* **deux** charts very carefully **et** learn these *(set)* **sept** *(moh)* **mots** now.

two   seven

I =	*(zhuh)* **je**	_____
you =	*(voo)* **vous**	_____
he =	*(eel)* **il**	_____
she =	*(el)* **elle**	_____

we =	*(noo)* **nous**	_____
they =	*(eel)* **ils** (♦ or mixed)	_____
they =	*(el)* **elles** (♦)	_____

Not too hard, is it? Draw lines between the matching **mots** *(ah⁽ⁿ⁾-glay)* **anglais et mots** *(frah⁽ⁿ⁾-say)* **français** below to

see if you can keep these **mots** straight in your mind.

(noo) **nous**   I

(eel) **ils**   they (♦)

(eel) **il**   you

(zhuh) **je**   he

(voo) **vous**   we

(el) **elle**   she

(el) **elles**   they (♦)

❏	**le marché** *(mar-shay)*	market
	– bon marché *(boh⁽ⁿ⁾)(mar-shay)*	inexpensive
❏	**le mariage** *(mah-ree-ahzh)*	marriage, wedding
❏	**le médicament** *(may-dee-kah-mah⁽ⁿ⁾)*	medicine **m**
❏	**la mer** *(mair)*	sea

Maintenant close **le livre et** write out both columns of this practice on a piece of **papier.** *(pah-pee-ay)* paper How did **vous** do? *(bya(n))* **Bien** *(mahl)* **ou mal?** well or poorly **Maintenant** that **vous** know these **mots, vous** can say almost you

anything **en français** with one basic formula: the "plug-in" formula.

To demonstrate, let's take **six** *(seess)* six basic **et** practical verbs **et** see how the "plug-in" formula works.

Write the verbs in the blanks after **vous** have practiced saying them out loud many times.

(par-lay) **parler** to speak _____

(ah-bee-tay) **habiter** to live, to reside *habiter, habiter* _____

(ah-shuh-tay) **acheter** to buy _____

(reh-stay) **rester** to remain, to stay _____

(koh-mah(n)-day) **commander** to order _____

(sah-puh-lay) **s'appeler** to be called _____

Besides the familiar words already circled, can **vous** find the above verbs in the puzzle below?

When **vous** find them, write them in the blanks to the right.

P	C	O	M	M	A	N	D	E	R	H
A	O	C	N	P	C	Q	U	I	E	A
R	M	D	O	Y	H	V	J	J	S	B
L	M	R	S	O	E	E	B	O	T	I
E	E	M	E	Ù	T	L	U	Y	E	T
R	N	D	I	R	E	T	M	N	R	E
V	T	N	I	L	R	B	D	E	I	R
S	'	A	P	P	E	L	E	R	H	T

1. _____

2. _____

3. _____

4. _____

5. _____

6. _____

❑	**le métro** *(may-troh)*	subway, metro	_____
❑	**la minute** *(mee-newt)*	minute	_____
	– la minuterie *(mee-new-tuh-ree)*	automatic light switch	_____
❑	**la mode** *(mohd)*	fashion **m**	_____
	– à la mode *(ah)(lah)(mohd)*	fashionable	

40

Study the following patterns carefully.

je *(zhuh)* **il** *(eel)* **elle** *(el)*	*(parl)* **parle**	=	I *speak* he/she *speaks*
	(ah-beet) **habite**	=	I *live* he/she *lives*
	(ah-shet) **achète**	=	I *buy* he/she *buys*
	(rest) **reste**	=	I *remain* he/she *remains*
	(koh-mah⁽ⁿ⁾d) **commande**	=	I *order* he/she *orders*
je	*(mah-pel)* **m'appelle**	=	I *am called*
il/elle	*(sah-pel)* **s'appelle**	=	he/she *is called*

nous *(noo)*	*(par-loh⁽ⁿ⁾)* **parlons**	=	we *speak*
	(zah-bee-toh⁽ⁿ⁾) **habitons**	=	we *live*
	(zah-shuh-toh⁽ⁿ⁾) **achetons**	=	we *buy*
	(reh-stoh⁽ⁿ⁾) **restons**	=	we *remain*
	(koh-mah⁽ⁿ⁾-doh⁽ⁿ⁾) **commandons**	=	we *order*
nous *(noo)*	**nous** *(noo)* **appelons** *(zah-puh-loh⁽ⁿ⁾)*	=	we *are called/ our name is*

Note:
- With all these verbs, the first thing you do is drop the final "**er**," "**ir**," or "**re**" from the basic verb form or stem.

- With "**je**," "**il**," or "**elle**," add "**e**" to the basic verb form.

- With "**nous**," add "**ons**."

- **S'appeler** varies but not too much. It is a very important verb so take a few extra minutes to learn it.

Some verbs just will not conform to the pattern! But don't worry. Speak slowly **et** clearly, **et** you will be perfectly understood whether you say "**parle**" or "**parlons.**" French speakers will be delighted that you have taken the time to learn their language.

Note:
- French has two separate and very different ways of saying "you" whereas in English we only use one word.

- "**Vous**" *(voo)* will be used throughout this book and will be appropriate for most situations. "**Vous**" refers to one person in a formal sense as well as being the plural in both a formal and informal sense. _{you}

- "**Tu**" *(too)* is a form of address reserved for family members and very close friends. _{you (singular)}

☐	**le monde** *(mohnd)*	world	
	– tout le monde *(too)(luh)(mohnd)*	everyone	
☐	**la montagne** *(moh⁽ⁿ⁾-tahn-yuh)*	mountain	**m**
☐	**le musée** *(mew-zay)*	museum	
☐	**la musique** *(mew-zeek)*	music	

Here's your next group of patterns!

(voo) **vous**	*(par-lay)* **parlez**	=	you *speak*	*(eel)* **ils** *(el)* **elles**	*(parl)* **parlent**	=	they *speak*
	(zah-bee-tay) **habitez**	=	you *live*		*(zah-beet)* **habitent**	=	they *live*
	(zah-shuh-tay) **achetez**	=	you *buy*		*(zah-shet)* **achètent**	=	they *buy*
	(reh-stay) **restez**	=	you *remain*		*(rest)* **restent**	=	they *remain*
	(koh-mah⁽ⁿ⁾-day) **commandez**	=	you *order*		*(koh-mah⁽ⁿ⁾d)* **commandent**	=	they *order*
(voo) **vous**	*(voo)* *(zah-puh-lay)* **vous appelez**	=	you *are called* / *your name is*	**ils/elles**	*(sah-pel)* **s'appellent**	=	they *are called* / *their name is*

Note:
- Notice that despite differences in spelling, many of the verbs are pronounced the same.
- With "**vous**," add "**ez**" to the basic verb form.
- With "**ils**," and "**elles**" simply add "**ent**" to the basic verb form. The "**ent**" is silent.

(vwah-lah) *(seess)*
Voilà six more verbs.
here are   six

(vuh-neer)
venir _____
to come

(ah-prah⁽ⁿ⁾-druh)
apprendre _____
to learn

(voo-dray)
voudrais _____
(I) would like

(ah-lay)
aller _____
to go

(ah-vwahr)
avoir _____ *avoir, avoir* _____
to have

(ah-vwahr) *(buh-zwa⁽ⁿ⁾)* *(duh)*
avoir besoin de _____
to need, to have need of

At the back of **le livre, vous** will find twelve

(pahzh)
pages of flash cards to help you learn these
pages
(noo-voh)
nouveaux mots. Cut them out; carry them in
new

your briefcase, purse, pocket *(oo)* **ou** knapsack; **et**
or

review them whenever **vous** have a free moment.

❏	**la nation** *(nah-syoh⁽ⁿ⁾)*	nation	_____
❏	**la nature** *(nah-tewr)*	nature	_____
❏	**naturel** *(nah-tew-rel)*	natural	**n** _____
	– au naturel *(oh)(nah-tew-rel)*	plain, simple	_____
❏	**la nécessité** *(nay-seh-see-tay)*	necessity	_____

42

Maintenant, it is your turn to practice what **vous** *(voo)* have learned. Fill in the following blanks with the correct form of the verb. Each time **vous** write out the sentence, be sure to say it aloud.

(par-lay)
parler
to speak

Bonjour!

Je _____ parle _____ français. *(frah⁽ⁿ⁾-say)*

Vous _____ parlez _____ anglais. *(ah⁽ⁿ⁾-glay)*

Il _____ parle _____ espagnol. *(eh-spahn-yohl)*
Elle parle — Spanish

Nous _____ parlons _____ japonais. *(zhah-poh-nay)*
— Japanese

Ils _____ parlent _____ allemand. *(ahl-mah⁽ⁿ⁾)* *(ahl-mah⁽ⁿ⁾)*
Elles parlent — German

(reh-stay)
rester
to remain, to stay

Je _____ reste _____ en France. *(frah⁽ⁿ⁾s)*

Vous restez/restez en Amérique. *(ah⁽ⁿ⁾-glay)*

Ils _____ restent _____ en Belgique. *(bel-zheek)*
Elles restent

Nous _____ restont _____ en Allemagne. *(ahl-mahn-yuh)*
— Germany

Ils _____ restent _____ en Espagne. *(eh-spahn-yuh)*
Elles restent — Spain

(ah-bee-tay)
habiter
to live, to reside

J' habite/ habite en France. *(frah⁽ⁿ⁾s)*

Vous _____ habitez _____ en Italie. *(ee-tah-lee)*

Il _____ habite _____ en Europe. *(uh-rohp)*
Elle habite

Nous _____ habitons _____ en Chine. *(sheen)*

Ils _____ habitent _____ en Japon. *(zhah-poh⁽ⁿ⁾)*
Elles habitent

(koh-mah⁽ⁿ⁾-day)
commander
to order

Je _____ commande _____ un verre de vin. *(vair)* *(va⁽ⁿ⁾)*

Vous _____ commandez _____ une tasse de thé. *(tahs)*

Il _____ commande _____ une tasse de café.
Elle commande

Nous _____ commandons _____ deux verres d'eau. *(duh)* *(vair)* *(doh)*
— water

Ils _____ commandent _____ trois verres de lait. *(twah)* *(lay)*
Elles commandent — milk

(ah-shuh-tay)
acheter
to buy

J' achète/ achète un livre. *(lee-vruh)*

Vous _____ achetez _____ une salade. *(sah-lahd)*

Il _____ achète _____ une horloge. *(or-lohzh)*
Elle achète — clock

Nous _____ achetons _____ trois tickets d'autobus. *(tee-kay)* *(doh-toh-boos)*

Ils _____ achètent _____ sept timbres. *(ta⁽ⁿ⁾-bruh)*
Elles achètent

(sah-puh-lay)
s'appeler
to be called

Je m'appelle Jeanne.

Je _____ m'appelle _____ Jeanne.

Vous _____ vous appellez _____ Mitou.

Il _____ s'appelle _____ Smith.
Elle s'appelle

Nous _____ nous appellons _____ Roquefort.

Ils _____ s'appellent _____ Vartan.
Elles s'appellent

❏	**neuf** *(nuf)*	new	_____
	– **Le Pont Neuf à Paris** *(poh⁽ⁿ⁾)(nuf)*	new bridge in Paris (1604)	_____
❏	**Noël** *(noh-el)*	Christmas	_____
❏	**le nord** *(nor)*	north	_____
❏	**Notre-Dame de Paris** *(noh-truh)(dahm)*	Our Lady of Paris (cathedral)	_____

n

Now take a break, walk around the room, take a deep breath **et** do the next **six** _(seess)_ verbs.

(vuh-neer)
venir
to come

Je __viens/_____ d'Amérique.

Vous __venez/_____ de Belgique.

Il __vient/_____ du Canada.
Elle

Nous __venons/_____ de New York.

Ils __viennent/_____ de *(swees)* **Suisse.**
Elles   Switzerland

(ah-lay)
aller
to go

Je __vais/_____ en France.

Vous __allez/_____ en *(ee-tah-lee)* **Italie.**

Il __va/_____ en Angleterre.
Elle

Nous __allons/_____ en *(bel-zheek)* **Belgique.**

Ils __vont/_____ en *(uh-rohp)* **Europe.**
Elles

(ah-prah⁽ⁿ⁾-druh)
apprendre
to learn

J'__apprends/_____ l'anglais.

Vous __apprenez/_____ le français.

Il __apprend/_____ l'italien.
Elle

Nous __apprenons/_____ l'allemand.

Ils __apprennent/_____ l'espagnol.
Elles   Spanish

(ah-vwahr)
avoir
to have

J'__ai/_____ *(deess)(uh-roh)* **dix euros.**

Vous __avez/_____ **cent euros.**

Il __a/_____ *(va⁽ⁿ⁾)* **vingt euros.**
Elle

Nous __avons/_____ *(sang-kah⁽ⁿ⁾t)* **cinquante euros.**

Ils __ont/_____ *(sank) (sah⁽ⁿ⁾)* **cinq cents euros.**
Elles

(voo-dray)
voudrais
(I) would like

Je __voudrais/_____ un *(vair)* *(va⁽ⁿ⁾)* **verre de vin.**

Vous __voudriez/_____ un verre de vin *(roozh)* **rouge.**

Il __voudrait/_____ deux verres de vin blanc.
Elle

Nous __voudrions/_____ trois *(vair)* **verres de vin.**

Ils __voudraient/_____ deux verres de *(lay)* **lait.**
Elles

(ah-vwahr)(buh-zwa⁽ⁿ⁾) (duh)
avoir besoin de
to have need of, to need

J'__ai besoin/_____ *(duh⁽ⁿ⁾)* *(doh)* **d'un verre d'eau.**

Vous _____ *(dewn)* **d'une tasse de thé.**

Il _____ de deux tasses de thé.
Elle

Nous _____ de trois tasses de café.

Ils _____ de cinq verres de bière.
Elles

❑ **l'objet** *(lohb-zhay)*	object	_____
❑ **obligatoire** *(oh-blee-gah-twahr)*	compulsory, obligatory	_____
❑ **l'observation** *(lohb-sair-vah-syoh⁽ⁿ⁾)*	observation **O**	_____
❑ **l'occupation** *(loh-kew-pah-syoh⁽ⁿ⁾)*	profession, occupation	_____
❑ **l'odeur** *(loh-dur)*	smell, odor	_____

Oui, *(wee)* yes it is hard to get used to all those **nouveaux** *(noo-voh)* **mots** *(moh)*. Just keep practicing **et** before **vous** *(voo)* know it, **vous** will be using them naturally. **Maintenant** is a perfect time to turn to the back of this **livre,** clip out your verb flash cards **et** start flashing. Don't skip over your free **mots** either. Check them off in the box provided as **vous apprenez** *(ah-preh-nay)* each one. See if **vous** can fill in the blanks below. **Les réponses correctes sont** at the bottom of **la page.**

1. _____
(I speak French.)

2. _____
(We learn French.)

3. _____
(She needs ten euros.)

4. _____
(He comes from Canada.)

5. _____
(They live in France.)

6. _____
(You buy a book.)

In the following Steps, **vous** will be introduced to more verbs **et vous** should drill them in exactly the same way as **vous** did in this section. Look up **les nouveaux mots** in your **dictionnaire** *(deek-syoh-nair)* dictionary **et** make up your own sentences. Try out your **nouveaux mots** for that's how you make them yours to use on your holiday. Remember, the more **vous** practice **maintenant,** the more enjoyable your trip will be. **Bonne** *(bun)* good **chance!** *(shah⁽ⁿ⁾s)* luck

(kel) *(uhr)* *(ay-teel)*
Quelle heure est-il?
what time is it

Vous know how to tell **les** *(zhoor)* **jours de la** *(suh-men)* **semaine et les** *(mwah)* **mois de l'année,** *(lah-nay)* so now let's learn to tell
days   week   months   year

time. As a *(vwah-yah-zhur)* **voyageur, vous** need to be able to tell time in order to make **réservations,**
          traveler

(rah⁽ⁿ⁾-day-voo)
rendez-vous et to catch **trains et autobus. Voilà les** "basics."
appointments   here are

What time is it?	=	*(kel)* *(uhr)* *(ay-teel)* **Quelle heure est-il?**
hour	=	*(uhr)* **heure**
noon	=	*(mee-dee)* **midi**
midnight	=	*(mee-nwee)* **minuit**
half past	=	*(duh-mee)* **et demie**
minus/less	=	*(mwa⁽ⁿ⁾)* **moins**
a quarter	=	*(kar)* **un quart**
a quarter to	=	*(mwa⁽ⁿ⁾)* *(kar)* **moins le quart**
a quarter after	=	*(kar)* **et quart**

Maintenant quiz yourself. Fill in the missing letters below.

midnight = `m i n u i t`   less = `m o i n s`

a quarter to = `m o i n s × l e × q u a r t`

half past = `e t × d e m i e`   hour = `h u e r e`

and finally   when = `q u a n d`

☐	**occupé** *(oh-kew-pay)*	busy, occupied	_____
	– **une ligne occupée**	engaged telephone line	_____
☐	**officiel** *(oh-fee-syel)*	official	_____
☐	**l'orchestre** *(lor-kess-truh)*	orchestra	_____
☐	**l'Orient** *(loh-ree-ah⁽ⁿ⁾)*	Orient	_____

o

Maintenant, comment *(koh-mah(n))* are these **mots** used? Study **les exemples** *(eg-zah(n)-pluh)* below. When **vous** think it
how   *examples*

through, it really is not too difficult. Just notice that the pattern changes after the halfway mark.

Notice that the phrase "o'clock" is not used in French.

Il est cinq heures. *(sank)* *(uhr)*
it is   five o'clock

5:00	Il est cinq heures.

Il est cinq heures dix. *(deess)*

5:10	Il est cinq heures dix.

Il est cinq heures et quart. *(kar)*
and a quarter

5:15	Il est cinq heures et quart.

Il est cinq heures vingt. *(va(n))*

5:20	Il est cinq heures vingt.

Il est cinq heures et demie. *(duh-mee)*
half past five

5:30	Il est cinq heures et demie.

Il est six heures moins vingt. *(seess)* *(mwa(n))*

5:40	Il est six heures moins vingt.

Il est six heures moins le quart.

5:45	Il est six heures moins le quart.

Il est six heures moins dix.

5:50	Il est six heures moins dix.

Il est six heures.

6:00	Il est six heures.

See how **important** it is to learn **les nombres**? *(nohm-bruh)* Answer the **questions** *(kes-tyoh(n))* **suivantes** *(swee-vah(n)t)* based on **les**
questions   *following*

horloges *(or-lohzh)* below. **Quelle** *(kel)* **heure** **est-il?** *(ay-teel)*
clocks

1. 8:00   Il est huit heures.

2. 7:15   Il est sept heures et quart.

3. 4:30   Il est quartre heures et demie.

4. 9:20   Il est neuf heures vingt.

47

When **vous** answer a "**Quand?**" (kah(n)) question, say "**à**" (ah) before **vous** give the time.
_{when} _{at}

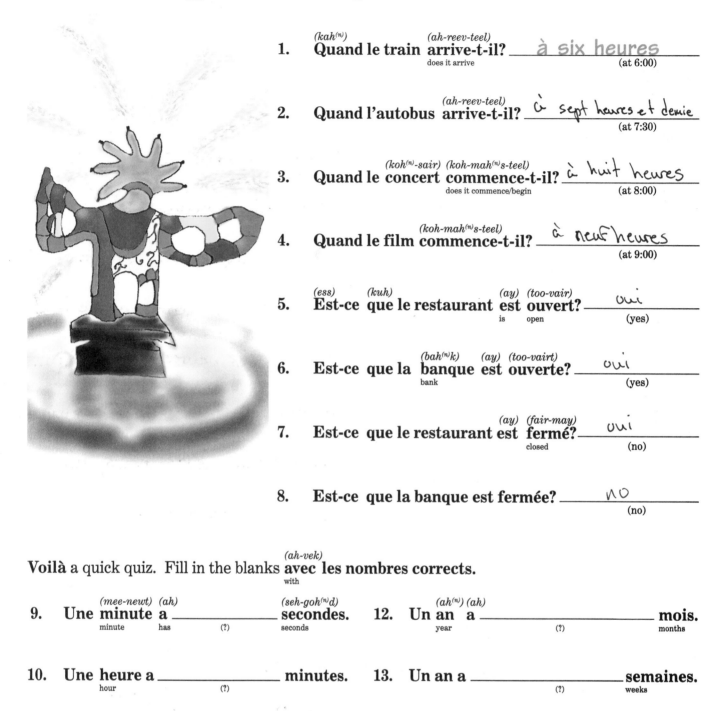

1. **Quand le train arrive-t-il?** (kah(n)) (ah-reev-teel) _____à six heures_____
   _{does it arrive} (at 6:00)

2. **Quand l'autobus arrive-t-il?** (ah-reev-teel) à sept heures et demie
   (at 7:30)

3. **Quand le concert commence-t-il?** (koh(n)-sair) (koh-mah(n)s-teel) à huit heures
   _{does it commence/begin} (at 8:00)

4. **Quand le film commence-t-il?** (koh-mah(n)s-teel) à neuf heures
   (at 9:00)

5. **Est-ce que le restaurant est ouvert?** (ess) (kuh) (ay) (too-vair) oui
   _{is} _{open} (yes)

6. **Est-ce que la banque est ouverte?** (bah(n)k) (ay) (too-vairt) oui
   _{bank} (yes)

7. **Est-ce que le restaurant est fermé?** (ay) (fair-may) oui
   _{closed} (no)

8. **Est-ce que la banque est fermée?** _____no_____
   (no)

Voilà a quick quiz. Fill in the blanks **avec** (ah-vek) **les nombres corrects.**
_{with}

9. **Une minute a** (mee-newt) (ah) _____ **secondes.**
   _{minute} _{has} _(?) _{seconds}

10. **Une heure a** _____ **minutes.**
    _{hour} _(?)

11. **Une semaine a** _____ **jours.**
    _{week} _(?) _{days}

12. **Un an a** (ah(n)) (ah) _____ **mois.**
    _{year} _(?) _{months}

13. **Un an a** _____ **semaines.**
    _(?) _{weeks}

14. **Un an a** _____ **jours.**
    _(?)

RÉPONSES

14. trois cent soixante-cinq	7. à cinq heures et demie
13. cinquante-deux	6. à huit heures et demie
12. douze	5. à onze heures et demie
11. sept	4. à neuf heures
10. soixante	3. à huit heures
9. soixante	2. à sept heures et demie
8. à une heure et demie	1. à six heures

48

Do **vous** remember your greetings from earlier? It is a good time to review them as they will

always be **très importantes.**
(za⁽ⁿ⁾-por-tah⁽ⁿ⁾-tuh) above importantes
very   important

À huit heures du matin on dit, "Bonjour, Madame Dupont."
(wheat) (uhr) (dew) (oh⁽ⁿ⁾)(dee) (mah-dahm) (dew-poh⁽ⁿ⁾)
at   morning   says   good morning   Mrs.

Qu'est-ce qu'on dit? ___Bonjour, Madame Dupont.___
(kess) (koh⁽ⁿ⁾) (dee)
what   does one   say

À une heure de l'après-midi on dit, "Bonjour, Monsieur Monet."
(ewn) (muh-syur)
one   afternoon   Mr.

Qu'est-ce qu'on dit? ___Bonjour, Monsieur Monet___
(kess) (koh⁽ⁿ⁾) (dee)

À huit heures du soir on dit, "Bonsoir, Mademoiselle Vartan."
(mahd-mwah-zel)
Miss

Qu'est-ce qu'on dit? ___Bonsoir, Mademoiselle Vartan___

À dix heures du soir on dit, "Bonne nuit, Monsieur Mitou."
(deess) (swahr) (bun) (nwee) (muh-syur)
ten   good   night

Qu'est-ce qu'on dit? ___Bonne nuit, Monsieur Mitou___

Vous have probably already noticed that plurals are *generally* formed by adding "s".

(vwah-tewr)	(lay) (vwah-tewr)
la voiture	**les voitures**
the car	the cars
(lee-vruh)	
le livre	**les livres**
book	books
(kart)	
la carte	**les cartes**
map	maps

Where to place the accent in French need never be a problem. **Les mots français** are always
(lay)   (frah⁽ⁿ⁾-say)

accented on the last syllable. It's easy. Don't be afraid of all the extra hyphens, apostrophes,

accents and uncommon squiggles in French. Concentrate on your easy pronunciation guide and

remember – practice, practice, practice.

(ess)	(kess) (kuh) (say)	(sah-pel)	(kess) (koh⁽ⁿ⁾)
est-ce	**qu'est-ce que c'est**	**il s'appelle**	**qu'est-ce qu'on**
is it	what is that	he is called	what does one

❏	**l'omelette** *(lohm-let)*	omelette	_____
❏	**on** *(oh⁽ⁿ⁾)*	one, people, they, we	_____
	– On fait ça. *(oh⁽ⁿ⁾)(fay)(sah)*	One does that. **o**	_____
	– On dit que . . . *(oh⁽ⁿ⁾)(dee)(kuh)*	One says that . . .	_____
❏	**l'optimiste** *(lohp-tee-meest)*	optimist	_____

Voilà deux new verbs **pour** Step 13.

(poor)
for

(mah⁽ⁿ⁾-zhay)
manger _____
to eat

(bwahr)
boire _____
to drink

(mah⁽ⁿ⁾-zhay)
manger
to eat

Je <u>mange/</u> _____ une salade. *(sah-lahd)*

Vous <u>mangez</u> _____ de la soupe. *(soup)* soup

Il <u>mange</u> _____ beaucoup. *(boh-koo)* very much
Elle

Nous <u>mangeons/</u> _____ des escargots. *(ess-kar-goh)* snails

Ils ne <u>mangent/</u> _____ rien. *(rya⁽ⁿ⁾)*
Elles

(bwahr)
boire
to drink

Je <u>bois/</u> _____ du lait. *(lay)*

Vous ne <u>buvez/</u> _____ rien. *(rya⁽ⁿ⁾)* nothing

Il <u>boit/</u> _____ du vin blanc.
Elle

Nous <u>buvons/</u> _____ des bières.

Ils <u>boivent/</u> _____ du thé.
Elles

Remember, to negate a statement, add "**ne**" before the verb and "**pas**" after the verb. Notice in *(nuh)* *(pah)*

the examples above, that when you used the word "**rien**," you also added "**ne**" before the verb. *(rya⁽ⁿ⁾)* nothing

(nuh) (mah⁽ⁿ⁾zh)
Je ne mange rien.
eat   nothing

Nous ne commandons rien.
we   order   nothing

(nuh) *(pah)*
Je ne parle pas français.
do not speak

Nous ne venons pas de Canada.
do not come

☐ **ordinaire** *(or-dee-nair)* . . . . ordinary _____

☐ **organisé** *(or-gah-nee-zay)* . . . . organized _____

☐ **l'origine** *(loh-ree-zheen)* . . . . origin _____ **O**

– Je suis d'origine américaine. . . . . I come from the USA originally. _____

☐ **l'ouest** *(luh-west)* . . . . west _____

Vous have learned a lot of material in the last few steps **et** that means it is time to quiz yourself. Don't panic, this is just for you **et** no one else needs to know how **vous** did. Remember, this is a chance to review, find out what **vous** remember **et** what **vous** need to spend more time on. After **vous** have finished, check your **réponses** in the glossary at the back of this book. Circle the correct answers.

le café	tea	(coffee)
oui	(yes)	no
la tante	(aunt)	uncle
ou	and	(or)
apprendre	to drink	(to learn)
la nuit	morning	(night)
vendredi	(Friday)	Tuesday
parler	to live	(to speak)
l'hiver	summer	(winter)
l'argent	(money)	page
dix	nine	(ten)
beaucoup	(a lot)	bread

la famille	seven	(family)
les enfants	(children)	grandfather
le lait	butter	(milk)
le sel	pepper	(salt)
sous	(under)	over
l'homme	(man)	doctor
juin	(June)	July
la cuisine	(kitchen)	religions
j'ai	I would like	(I have)
acheter	to order	(to buy)
hier	(yesterday)	tomorrow
bon	(good)	yellow

(koh-mah⁽ⁿ⁾) *(tah-lay-voo)*
Comment allez-vous?   <u>What time is it?</u>   <u>How are you?</u>   Well, how are you after this quiz?

❐ **la paire** *(pair)*	pair	_____
❐ **le pantalon** *(pah⁽ⁿ⁾-tah-loh⁽ⁿ⁾)*	pair of trousers	_____
❐ **le Pape** *(pahp)*	Pope	_____
❐ **parfait** *(par-fay)*	perfect	_____
– **C'est parfait.** *(say)(par-fay)*	That's fine.	

p

51

14 *(nor)* *(sood)* *(est)* *(west)*
Nord - Sud, Est - Ouest
north   south   east   west

If **vous** are looking at **une** *(kart)* **carte et vous** see **les mots** *(swee-vah⁽ⁿ⁾)* **suivants**, it should not be too difficult to
map
figure out what they mean. Take an educated guess.

(lah-may-reek) *(dew)* *(nor)*   *(pohl)*
l'Amérique du nord   **le Pôle nord**

(dew) *(sood)*   *(pohl)*
l'Amérique du sud   **le Pôle sud**

(koht) *(duh)* *(lest)*   *(lah-freek)*
la côte de l'est   **l'Afrique du sud**

(luh-west)   *(leer-lahnd)* *(nor)*
la côte de l'ouest   **l'Irelande du nord**

Les mots français pour "north," "south," "east," **et** "west" are easy to recognize due to their

similarity to **anglais**. These **mots sont** *(treh)* **très** *(za⁽ⁿ⁾-por-tah⁽ⁿ⁾)* **importants**. Learn them **aujourd'hui!**
are

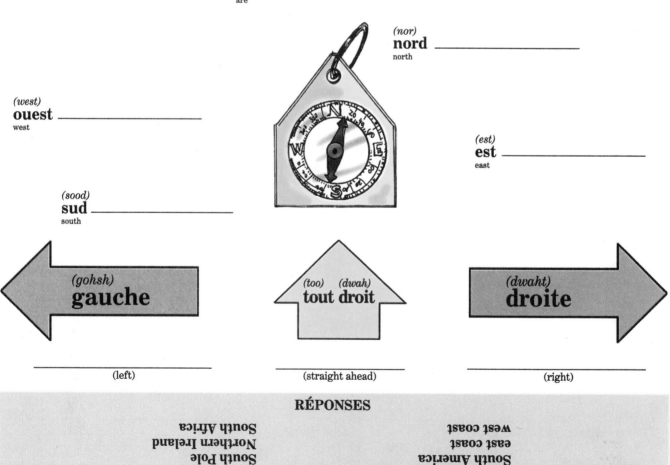

(nor)
nord _____
north

(west)
ouest _____
west

(est)
est _____
east

(sood)
sud _____
south

(gohsh)
gauche

(too) *(dwah)*
tout droit

(dwaht)
droite

_____   _____   _____
(left)   (straight ahead)   (right)

These **mots** can go a long way. Say them aloud each time you write them in the blanks below.

(seel) (voo)   (play)
s'il vous plaît _____ s'il vous plaît _____
please

(mair-see)
merci _____ merci _____
thank you

(par-doh$^{(n)}$) (ek-skew-zay-mwah)
pardon/excusez-moi _____ pardon/excusez-moi _____
excuse me

(duh)(rya$^{(n)}$)
de rien _____ de rien _____
you're welcome

Voilà deux *(koh$^{(n)}$-vair-sah-syoh$^{(n)}$)* **conversations très** *(tee-peek)* **typiques pour** someone who is trying to find something. Write
two   conversations   very   typical   for

them out in the blanks below.

Jean Paul: **Excusez-moi, mais où est** *(may)* **l'Hôtel Cézanne?** *(loh-tel)*
but

_____ **Excusez-moi, mais où est l'Hôtel Cézanne?** _____

Claude: *(koh$^{(n)}$-tee-new-ay)* **Continuez tout droit.** *(toor-nay)* **Tournez à gauche à la deuxième rue.** *(duh-zee-em) (rew)*
continue   turn   to the left   second   street

_____ Continuez tout droit. Tournez à gauche à la
douxième rue. _____

L'Hôtel Cézanne est à droite.
on the right

_____ L'Hôtel Cézanne est à droite. _____

Thomas: **Pardon, Monsieur. Où est le Musée d'Orsay?** *(moo-zay) (dor-say)*
museum

_____ Pardon Monsieur. Où est le Musée d'Orsay? _____

Christine: *(toor-nay)* **Tournez à droite ici.** *(ee-see)* **Continuez environ** *(ah$^{(n)}$-vee-roh$^{(n)}$)* **cent mètres.** *(sah$^{(n)}$) (meh-truh)*
turn   here   about   meters

_____ Tournez à droite ici. Continuez environ cent mètres. _____

Le Musée d'Orsay est à gauche.
on the left

_____ Le Musée d'Orsay est à gauche. _____

☐ **le parc** *(park)* . . . . park _____
☐ **le parfum** *(par-fuh$^{(n)}$)* . . . . perfume _____
– **la parfumerie** *(par-few-muh-ree)* . . . . perfume shop **p** _____
☐ **le parking** *(par-keeng)* . . . . parking lot _____
☐ **le passeport** *(pahs-por)* . . . . passport _____

53

Are **vous** lost? There is no need to be lost if **vous** **avez** *(voo)* *(zah-vay)* learned the basic **mots de direction.** *(dee-rek-syoh⁽ⁿ⁾)*
have

Do not try to memorize these **conversations** because **vous** will never be looking for precisely

these places. One day, **vous** might need to ask for **directions** to "**le Louvre**" *(loo-vruh)* or "**l'Hôtel**

Maurice." Learn the key direction **mots et** be sure **vous** can find your destination. **Vous** may

want to buy a guidebook to start planning which places **vous** would like to visit. Practice asking

directions to these special places. What if the person responding to your **question** answers too

quickly for **vous** to understand the entire reply? Practice saying,

Pardon. Je ne comprends pas. Répétez, s'il vous plaît. Merci.
(zhuh) (nuh)(koh⁽ⁿ⁾-prah⁽ⁿ⁾) (pah) (ray-pay-tay)
do not understand   repeat

Maintenant, say it again **et** then write it out below.

Pardon. Je ne comprends pas. Répétez, s'il vous plaît. Merci.

(Excuse me. I do not understand. Please repeat. Thank you.)

Oui, c'est difficile at first but don't give up! **Quand** the directions are repeated, **vous** will be able
(wee) *(dee-fee-seel)* *(voo)* *(zah-vay)*
yes   difficult   when

to understand if **vous** **avez** learned the key **mots.** Let's review by writing them in the blanks below.

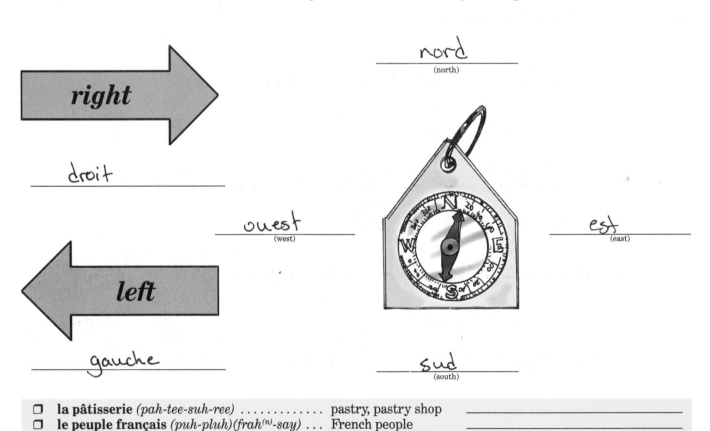

right

droit

left

gauche

nord
(north)

ouest
(west)

est
(east)

sud
(south)

☐ **la pâtisserie** *(pah-tee-suh-ree)*	pastry, pastry shop	_____
☐ **le peuple français** *(puh-pluh)(frah⁽ⁿ⁾-say)* . . .	French people	_____
☐ **la pharmacie** *(far-mah-see)*	pharmacy **p**	_____
☐ **la photo** *(foh-toh)*	photo	_____
☐ **la pilule** *(pee-lewl)*	pill	_____

(vwah-lah) (kah-truh) (noo-voh)
Voilà quatre nouveaux verbes.
_{new}

(deer)
dire _____ dire _____
to say

(koh(n)-prah(n)-druh)
comprendre _____ comprendre _____
to understand

(vah(n)-druh)
vendre _____ vendre _____
to sell

(ray-pay-tay)
répéter _____ répéter _____
to repeat

As always, say each sentence out loud. Say each **et** every **mot** carefully, pronouncing each

French sound as well as **vous** can.

(deer)
dire
to say

Je _dis/_____ "Bonjour."

Vous _dites/_____ *(noh(n))* "Non."
_{no}

Il _dit/_____ *(sah-lew)* "Salut."
Elle

Nous _disons/_____ *(wee)* "Oui."

Ils ne _disent/_____ *(rya(n))* rien.
Elles _{nothing}

(koh(n)-prah(n)-druh)
comprendre
to understand

Je _comprends/_____ *(lah(n)-glay)* l'anglais.

Vous _____ *(lee-tah-lya(n))* l'italien.

Il _____ *(lahl-mah(n))* l'allemand.
Elle

Nous _comprenons/_____ *(roos)* le russe.
_{Russian}

Ils _____ le français.
Elles _{French}

Je _vends/_____ *(day)* des fleurs.
_{some}

Vous ne _____ *(rya(n))* rien.

Il _vend/_____ des cartes postales.
Elle _{postcards}

Nous _____ *(fwee)* des fruits.

Ils _____ *(ta(n)-bruh)* des timbres.
Elles

(ray-pay-tay)
répéter Que? Que? Que?
to repeat

Je _répète/_____ le mot.

Vous _répétez/_____ la réponse.

Il _répète/_____ *(noh(n))* les noms.
Elle _{names}

Nous _répétons/_____ les questions.
_{questions}

Ils ne _répètent/_____ rien.
Elles

❐ **le pique-nique** *(peek-neek)*	picnic	_____
❐ **la place** *(plahs)*	place, seat, square (in a town)	_____
❐ **le plaisir** *(play-zeer)*	pleasure	_____
– **Avec plaisir** *(ah-vek)(play-zeer)*	with pleasure **p**	
❐ **la police** *(poh-lees)*	police	

55

(noo) (zah-loh⁽ⁿ⁾)(ah⁽ⁿ⁾-kor)   *(maze-oh⁽ⁿ⁾)*
Maintenant nous allons encore apprendre des mots. Voilà une maison en France. Go to
more   learn   house

(shah⁽ⁿ⁾-bruh) (koo-shay)   *(pyess)*   *(noh⁽ⁿ⁾)*
your **chambre à coucher et** look around **la pièce.** Let's learn **les noms** of the things **dans**
bedroom   room   names

(noo)
la chambre, just like **nous** learned the various parts of **la maison.**

(shah⁽ⁿ⁾-bruh)   (koo-shay)   (ah⁽ⁿ⁾) (oh)
La chambre à coucher est en haut.
bedroom   upstairs

(lar-mwahr)
l'armoire _____
wardrobe

(lee)
le lit _____
bed

(loh-ray-yay)
l'oreiller _____
pillow

(koo-vair-tewr)
la couverture _____
blanket

(ray-vay)
le réveil _____
alarm clock

(sah-loh⁽ⁿ⁾)   (bah)
Le salon est en bas.
living room   downstairs

_____ _____ **est la chambre à coucher?**
(where)   (where)

☐ **la politesse** *(poh-lee-tess)*	politeness	
☐ **la politique** *(poh-lee-teek)*	politics	**p** _____
☐ **le port** *(por)*	port	_____
☐ **la Préfecture de Police** *(pray-fek-tewr)*	Police Headquarters	_____
☐ **premier** *(pruh-mee-air)*	first	_____

Maintenant, remove the next *(sank)* **cinq** stickers **et** label these things **dans** your **chambre à coucher.**

Let's move into **la salle de bains** *(sahl)* *(ba⁽ⁿ⁾)* **et** do the same thing. Remember, **la salle de bains** *(ba⁽ⁿ⁾)* means a
bathroom

room to bathe in. If **vous** *(voo)* **êtes dans un restaurant et vous** *(zet)* need to use the lavatory,

vous want to ask for **les toilettes** *(twah-let)* *not* for **la salle de bains.** Restrooms

may be marked with pictures **ou** simply with the letters **D** **ou** **M.**

Don't confuse them!

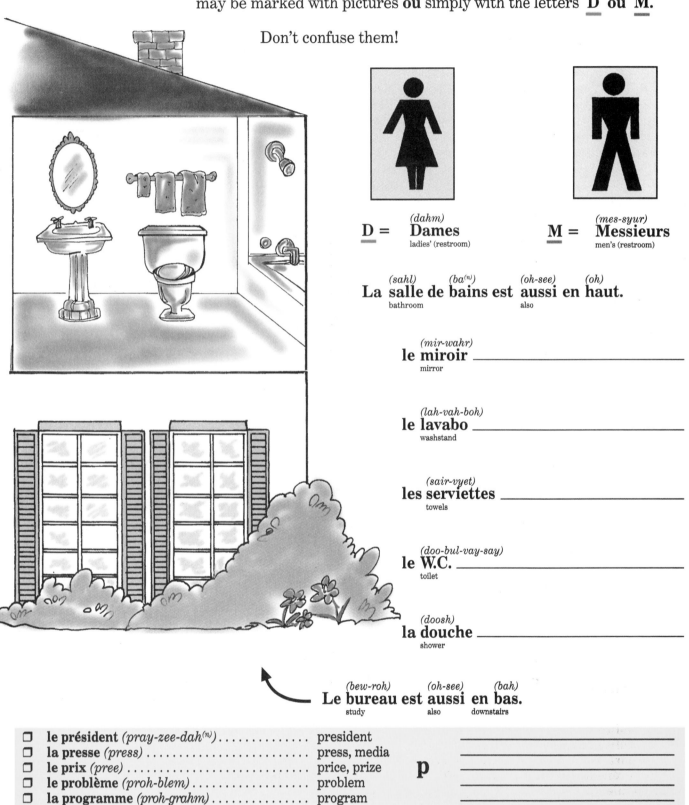

D = **Dames** *(dahm)*
ladies' (restroom)

M = **Messieurs** *(mes-syur)*
men's (restroom)

La salle de bains est *(sahl)* *(ba⁽ⁿ⁾)* **aussi en haut.** *(oh-see)* *(oh)*
bathroom   also

le miroir *(mir-wahr)* _____
mirror

le lavabo *(lah-vah-boh)* _____
washstand

les serviettes *(sair-vyet)* _____
towels

le W.C. *(doo-bul-vay-say)* _____
toilet

la douche *(doosh)* _____
shower

Le bureau est aussi en bas. *(bew-roh)* *(oh-see)* *(bah)*
study   also   downstairs

❑ **le président** *(pray-zee-dah⁽ⁿ⁾)*	president	_____
❑ **la presse** *(press)*	press, media	_____
❑ **le prix** *(pree)*	price, prize	**p** _____
❑ **le problème** *(proh-blem)*	problem	_____
❑ **la programme** *(proh-grahm)*	program	_____

Do not forget to remove the next group of stickers **et** label these things in your **maison** (may-zoh(n)). Okay, it is time to review. Here's a quick quiz to see what you remember.

men's (restroom)   *(bah)* **en bas**

I understand   *(mes-syur)* **messieurs**

downstairs   *(seel) (voo) (play)* **s'il vous plaît**

please   *(koh(n)-prah(n))* **je comprends**

towels   *(sahl) (ba(n))* **la salle de bains**

upstairs   *(too) (dwah)* **tout droit**

bathroom   *(dahm)* **dames**

lavatory/restroom   *(sair-vyet)* **les serviettes**

straight ahead   *(oh)* **en haut**

women's (restroom)   *(twah-let)* **les toilettes**

Next stop — **le bureau,** specifically **la table** ou le **bureau dans le bureau. Qu'est-ce qu'il y a**
(bew-roh) office   *(tah-bluh)* table   *(bew-roh)* desk   *(kess)* what   *(keel-yah)* is there

sur le bureau? Let's identify **les choses** which one normally finds **sur le bureau** or strewn
on   things

about **la maison.**

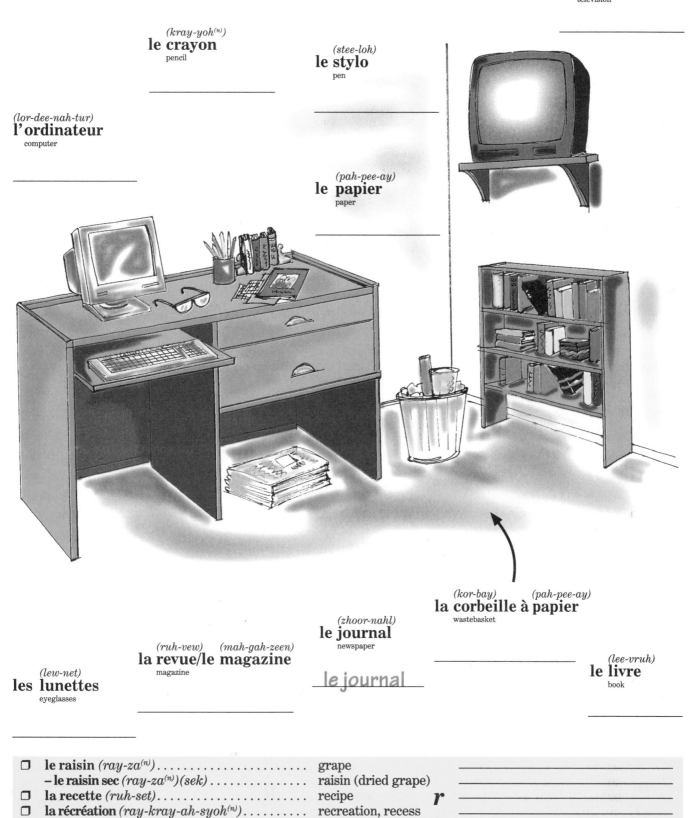

(tay-lay-vee-syoh[n])
la télévision
television

(kray-yoh[n])
le crayon
pencil

(stee-loh)
le stylo
pen

(lor-dee-nah-tur)
l'ordinateur
computer

(pah-pee-ay)
le papier
paper

(kor-bay) **(pah-pee-ay)**
la corbeille à papier
wastebasket

(zhoor-nahl)
le journal
newspaper

le journal

(ruh-vew) **(mah-gah-zeen)**
la revue/le magazine
magazine

(lew-net)
les lunettes
eyeglasses

(lee-vruh)
le livre
book

59

Don't forget these essentials!

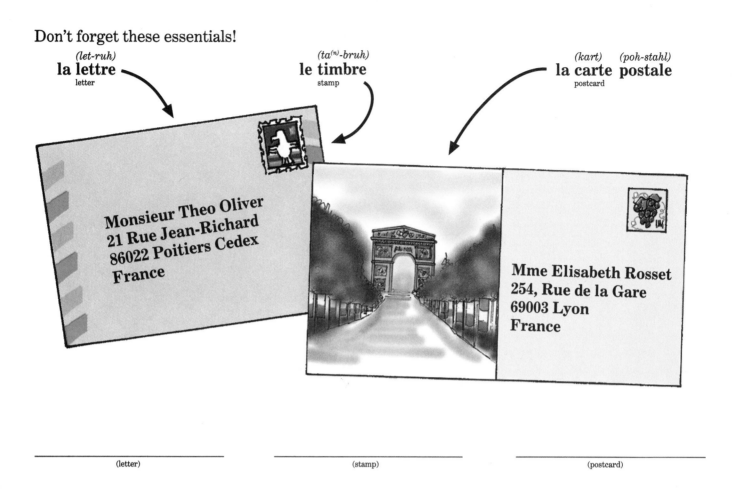

(let-ruh)
la lettre
letter

(ta⁽ⁿ⁾-bruh)
le timbre
stamp

(kart) (poh-stahl)
la carte postale
postcard

Monsieur Theo Oliver
21 Rue Jean-Richard
86022 Poitiers Cedex
France

Mme Elisabeth Rosset
254, Rue de la Gare
69003 Lyon
France

_____
(letter)

_____
(stamp)

_____
(postcard)

Remember that "**oi**" sounds like "wah." Practice this sound **avec les mots suivants:**

(bwah) *(bwah)*   *(ah⁽ⁿ⁾-vwah)* *(ah⁽ⁿ⁾-vwah)*
bois, boit, trois, soixante, mademoiselle, poivre, bonsoir, envoie and **envoient.**
drink drinks three   pepper   send   send

Notice that "**ent**" at the end of a verb is silent: *(parl)* **parle** and *(parl)* **parlent**, *(mah⁽ⁿ⁾zh)* **mange** and *(mah⁽ⁿ⁾zh)* **mangent**.
                  speak   speaks   eat   eat

(ness) *(pah)* *(ek-streh-muh-mah⁽ⁿ⁾)*
The expression "**n'est-ce pas**" is **extrêmement** useful **en français.** Added onto a sentence, it
                extremely

turns the sentence into a question for which **la réponse** is usually "**oui.**" It has only one form

and is much simpler than **en anglais.**

(ness) *(pah)*
C'est un livre, n'est-ce pas?   =   It's a book, isn't it?

(bel)
Jacqueline est belle, n'est-ce pas?   =   Jacqueline is beautiful, isn't she?

(voo) (zet)
Vous êtes français, n'est-ce pas?   =   You're French, aren't you?

❐	**la Renaissance** *(ruh-nay-sah⁽ⁿ⁾s)*	rebirth, the Renaissance	_____
❐	**le rendez-vous** *(rah⁽ⁿ⁾-day-voo)*	rendezvous, appointment	_____
❐	**la république** *(ray-pew-bleek)*	republic	_____
	– **La Cinquième République** (1958-) . . .	the Fifth Republic **r**	_____
❐	**la réservation** *(ray-zair-vah-syoh⁽ⁿ⁾)*	reservation	

Simple, isn't it? **Maintenant,** after you fill in the blanks below, go back a second time and negate all these sentences by adding **"ne"** before each verb and **"pas"** after each verb. Don't get discouraged! Just look at how much **vous** have already learned **et** think ahead to wonderful food, **la Tour** *(toor)* **Eiffel** *(ee-fel)* **et** new adventures.

(vwahr)
voir _____
to see

(dor-meer)
dormir _____
to sleep

(ahⁿ-vwhy-ay)
envoyer _____
to send

(shair-shay)
chercher _____
to look for

(vwahr)
voir
to see

Je __vois/_____ le **marché.** *(mar-shay)* market

Vous __voyez/_____ le **Louvre.** *(loo-vruh)*

Il __voit/_____ la **Tour Eiffel.** *(toor) (ee-fel)*
Elle

Nous __voyons/_____ le **Pont Neuf.** *(pohⁿ) (nuf)* bridge

Ils __voient/_____ **Notre-Dame.**
Elles

(dor-meer)
dormir
to sleep

Je __dors/_____ dans la **chambre.** *(shahⁿ-bruh)*

Vous __dormez/_____ dans l'**hôtel.**

Il __dort/_____ dans la **maison.**
Elle

Nous _____ sous la **couverture.** *(800)* blanket

Ils _____ **sans oreillers.** *(sahⁿ)* without pillows
Elles

(ahⁿ-vwhy-ay)
envoyer
to send

J' __envoie/_____ la **lettre.** letter

Vous __envoyez/_____ la **carte postale.**

Il __envoie/_____ le **livre.**
Elle

Nous _____ quatre **cartes postales.** *(kah-truh)*

Ils __envoient/_____ trois **lettres.**
Elles

(shair-shay)
chercher
to look for

Je _____ le **Louvre.**

Vous __cherchez/_____ les **lunettes.** *(lew-net)*

Il _____ le **Musée d'Orsay.**
Elle

Nous _____ l'**Opéra.**

Ils _____ l' **Hôtel de Ville.** *(veel)* town hall
Elles

❏ **la résidence** *(ray-zee-dahⁿs)*	residence	
❏ **la résistance** *(ray-zee-stahⁿs)*	resistance	
❏ **la révolution** *(ray-voh-lew-syohⁿ)*	revolution **r**	
– 1789 - **la Révolution française**	French Revolution	
❏ **la route** *(root)*	route, highway	

Before **vous** proceed with the next step, *(seel)* *(voo)* *(play)* s'il vous plaît, identify all the items **en bas**.

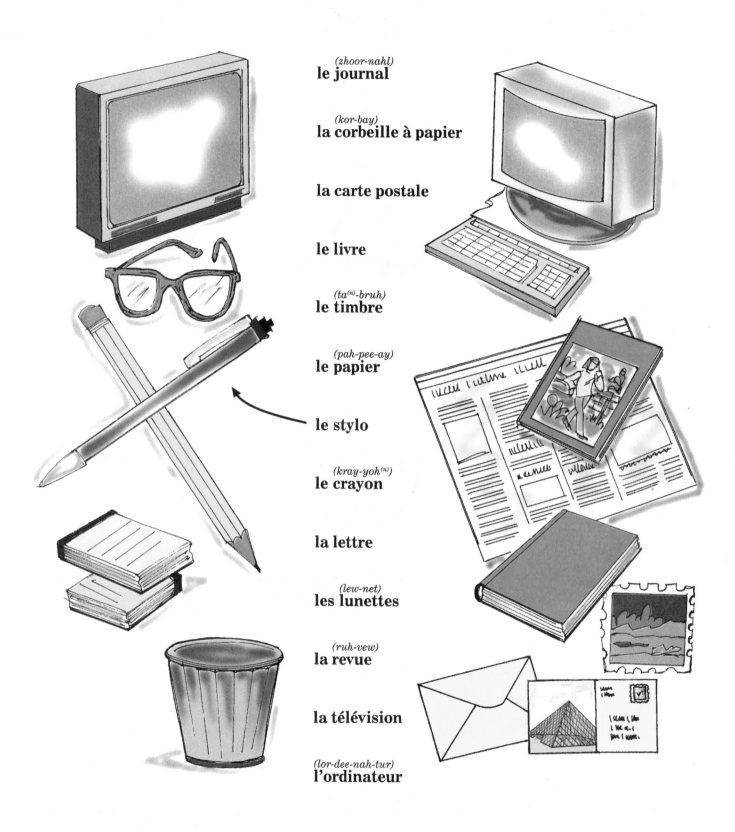

(zhoor-nahl)
le **journal**

(kor-bay)
la **corbeille à papier**

la **carte postale**

le **livre**

(ta⁽ⁿ⁾-bruh)
le **timbre**

(pah-pee-ay)
le **papier**

le stylo

(kray-yoh⁽ⁿ⁾)
le **crayon**

la **lettre**

(lew-net)
les **lunettes**

(ruh-vew)
la **revue**

la **télévision**

(lor-dee-nah-tur)
l'**ordinateur**

☐	le sac *(sack)*	sack		
☐	sacré *(sah-kray)*	sacred	**S**	
	– Sacré-Coeur à Paris *(sah-kray-kur)*	Sacred Heart (church in Paris)		
☐	sage *(sahzh)*	wise, well-behaved		
☐	la saison *(say-zoh⁽ⁿ⁾)*	season		

Maintenant vous know how to count, how to ask **questions**, how to use **verbes avec** the "plug-in"

formula **et** how to describe something, be it the location of **un hôtel ou la couleur d'une maison.** *(dewn)*

house

Let's take the basics that **vous** have learned **et** expand them in special areas that will be most

helpful in your travels. What does everyone do on a holiday? Send postcards, **n'est-ce pas?** *(ness) (pah)*

Let's learn exactly how **le bureau de poste (la Poste)** works. *(bew-roh) (pohst)*

post office

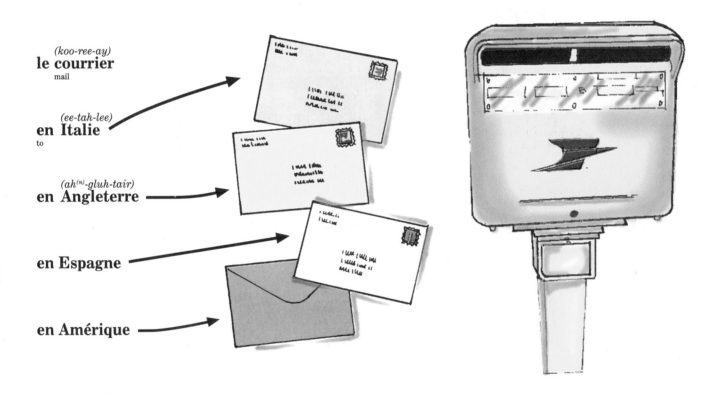

le courrier *(koo-ree-ay)*

mail

en Italie *(ee-tah-lee)*

to

en Angleterre *(ah⁽ⁿ⁾-gluh-tair)*

en Espagne

en Amérique

Les P.T.T. *(lay) (pay-tay-tay)* **ou la Poste** is where **vous** buy **les timbres,** send **des paquets et des cartes** *(pah-kay)*

packages

postales. Les P.T.T ont tout. *(ah⁽ⁿ⁾) (too)*

have   everything

❏	**les salutations** *(sah-lew-tah-syoh⁽ⁿ⁾)*	greeting	_____
❏	**le sandwich** *(sah⁽ⁿ⁾-dweech)*	sandwich	_____
❏	**la sauce** *(sohs)*	sauce **s**	_____
❏	**le saumon** *(soh-moh⁽ⁿ⁾)*	salmon	_____
❏	**la science** *(see-ah⁽ⁿ⁾s)*	science	_____

Voilà the necessary **mots pour le bureau de poste.** Practice them aloud **et** write them in the blanks.

(let-ruh)
la lettre
letter

(kart) (poh-stahl)
la carte postale
postcard

(pah-kay)
le paquet
package

(mail) (lay-mail)
le mel / l'email
email

(par) (ah-vyoh⁽ⁿ⁾)
par avion
by airmail

(fahx)
le fax

(ta⁽ⁿ⁾-bruh)
le timbre
stamp

(kah-been) (tay-lay-foh-neek)
la cabine téléphonique
telephone booth

(bwaht) (oh) (let-ruh)
la boîte aux lettres
mailbox

(tay-lay-fohn)
le téléphone

Next step — **vous** ask **questions** like those **en bas,** depending on what **vous voudriez.** *(voo-dree-ay)* would like Repeat these sentences aloud many times.

(oo) (ess) (koh⁽ⁿ⁾) (nah-shet)
Où est-ce qu'on achète des timbres? _____
does one buy

Où est-ce qu'on achète une carte postale? _____

(koh⁽ⁿ⁾) (tay-lay-fohn)
Où est-ce qu'on téléphone? _____
does one telephone

(ay) (bwaht) (oh)
Où est la boîte aux lettres? _____
is

(ay) (kah-been) (tay-lay-foh-neek)
Où est la cabine téléphonique? _____
is

(ess) (koh⁽ⁿ⁾) (nah⁽ⁿ⁾-vwah)
Où est-ce qu'on envoie un paquet? _____
does one send

(nah⁽ⁿ⁾-vwah) (mail)
Où est-ce qu'on envoie un mel? _____

(kohm-bya⁽ⁿ⁾) (sah) (koot)
Combien ça coûte? _____

Maintenant, quiz yourself. See if **vous** can translate the following thoughts **en français.**

1. Where is the telephone booth? _____

2. Where does one telephone? _____

3. Where is the mailbox? _____

4. Where is the post office? _____

5. Where does one buy stamps? _____

6. How much is it? _____

7. Where does one send a package? _____

8. Where does one send a fax? _____

65

Voilà quatre nouveaux verbes.

(fair)
faire _____
to make, to do

(moh⁽ⁿ⁾-tray)
montrer _____
to show

(ay-kreer)
écrire _____
to write

(pay-yay)
payer _____
to pay

Practice these verbs by not only filling in the blanks, but by saying them aloud many, many

times until you are comfortable with the sounds **et** the words.

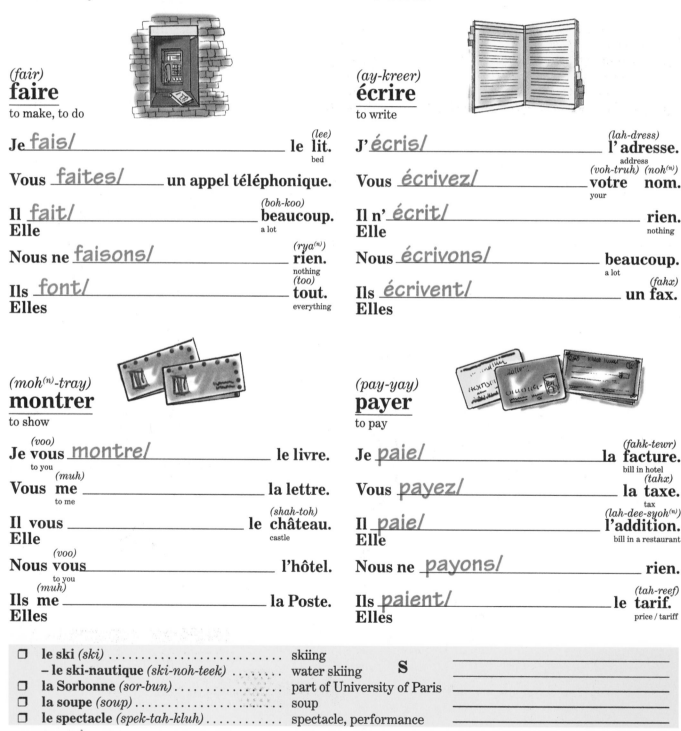

(fair)
faire
to make, to do

Je _fais/_ _____ le **lit.** *(lee)* bed

Vous _faites/_ _____ **un appel téléphonique.**

Il _fait/_ _____ **beaucoup.** *(boh-koo)* a lot
Elle

Nous ne _faisons/_ _____ **rien.** *(rya⁽ⁿ⁾)* nothing

Ils _font/_ _____ **tout.** *(too)* everything
Elles

(ay-kreer)
écrire
to write

J' _écris/_ _____ **l'adresse.** *(lah-dress)* address

Vous _écrivez/_ _____ **votre nom.** *(voh-truh) (noh⁽ⁿ⁾)* your

Il n' _écrit/_ _____ **rien.** nothing
Elle

Nous _écrivons/_ _____ **beaucoup.** a lot

Ils _écrivent/_ _____ **un fax.** *(fahx)*
Elles

(moh⁽ⁿ⁾-tray)
montrer
to show

Je vous _montre/_ _____ **le livre.** *(voo)* to you

Vous me _____ **la lettre.** *(muh)* to me

Il vous _____ **le château.** *(shah-toh)* castle
Elle

Nous vous _____ **l'hôtel.** *(voo)* to you

Ils me _____ **la Poste.** *(muh)*
Elles

(pay-yay)
payer
to pay

Je _paie/_ _____ **la facture.** *(fahk-tewr)* bill in hotel

Vous _payez/_ _____ **la taxe.** *(tahx)* tax

Il _paie/_ _____ **l'addition.** *(lah-dee-syoh⁽ⁿ⁾)* bill in a restaurant
Elle

Nous ne _payons/_ _____ **rien.**

Ils _paient/_ _____ **le tarif.** *(tah-reef)* price / tariff
Elles

❐ **le ski** *(ski)*	skiing	**S** _____
– **le ski-nautique** *(ski-noh-teek)*	water skiing	_____
❐ **la Sorbonne** *(sor-bun)*	part of University of Paris	_____
❐ **la soupe** *(soup)*	soup	_____
❐ **le spectacle** *(spek-tah-kluh)*	spectacle, performance	_____

Some of these signs you probably recognize, but take a couple of minutes to review them anyway.

(seer-kew-lah-syoh$^{(n)}$) *(a$^{(n)}$-tair-deet)*
circulation interdite
road closed to vehicles

(doo-ahn)
douane
customs

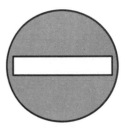

(ahk-seh) *(a$^{(n)}$-tair-dee)*
accès interdit
no entrance

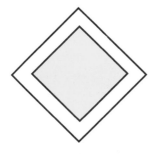

(pree-or-ee-tay) *(pah-sahzh)*
priorité de passage
main road, you have the right of way

(say-day)
cédez le passage
yield

(lee-mee-tah-syoh$^{(n)}$) *(vee-tess)*
limitation de vitesse
speed limit

(stah-see-oh$^{(n)}$-nuh-mah$^{(n)}$) *(a$^{(n)}$-tair-dee)*
stationnement interdit
no parking

(a$^{(n)}$-tair-dee)
passage interdit
no passing

(stohp)
stop
stop

(day-vee-ah-syoh$^{(n)}$)
DÉVIATION
detour

What follows are approximate conversions, so when you order something by liters, kilograms or grams you will have an idea of what to expect and not find yourself being handed one piece of candy when you thought you ordered an entire bag.

To Convert		Do the Math		
liters (l) to gallons,	multiply by 0.26	4 liters x 0.26	=	1.04 gallons
gallons to liters,	multiply by 3.79	10 gal. x 3.79	=	37.9 liters
kilograms (kg) to pounds,	multiply by 2.2	2 kilograms x 2.2	=	4.4 pounds
pounds to kilos,	multiply by 0.46	10 pounds x 0.46	=	4.6 kg
grams (g) to ounces,	multiply by 0.035	100 grams x 0.035	=	3.5 oz.
ounces to grams,	multiply by 28.35	10 oz. x 28.35	=	283.5 g.
meters (m) to feet,	multiply by 3.28	2 meters x 3.28	=	6.56 feet
feet to meters,	multiply by 0.3	6 feet x 0.3	=	1.8 meters

For fun, take your weight in pounds and convert it into kilograms. It sounds better that way, doesn't it? How many kilometers is it from your home to school, to work, to the post office?

The Simple Versions		
one liter	=	approximately one US quart
four liters	=	approximately one US gallon
one kilo	=	approximately 2.2 pounds
100 grams	=	approximately 3.5 ounces
500 grams	=	slightly more than one pound
one meter	=	slightly more than three feet

The distance between **New York et Paris** is approximately 3,622 miles. How many kilometers would that be? It is 215 miles between **Londres et Paris**. How many kilometers is that?

kilometers (km.) to miles,	multiply by 0.62	1000 km. x 0.62	=	620 miles
miles to kilometers,	multiply by 1.6	1000 miles x 1.6	=	1,600 km.

Inches	1		2		3		4		5		6		7

To convert centimeters into inches, multiply by 0.39   Example: 9 cm. x 0.39   = 3.51 in.

To convert inches into centimeters, multiply by 2.54   Example: 4 in. x 2.54   = 10.16 cm.

cm 1	2	3	4	5	6	7	8	9	10	11	12	13	14	15	16	17	18

18

(koh-mah⁽ⁿ⁾) *(pay-yay)*

Comment Payer
how   to pay

Oui, il y a aussi bills to pay **en France. Vous** have just finished your **repas délicieux et**
(eel-yah) *(oh-see)*   *(ruh-pah)* *(day-lee-syuh)*
there are   also   meal   delicious

vous voudriez l'addition. Que faites-vous? Vous call for **le garçon (monsieur!) ou la**
(voo-dree-ay) *(lah-dee-syoh⁽ⁿ⁾)*   *(fet-voo)*   *(gar-soh⁽ⁿ⁾)*
would like   bill   do you do   waiter

serveuse (mademoiselle! ou madame!). Le garçon will normally reel off what **vous avez**
(sair-vuz)   *(zah-vay)*
waitress   have

eaten while writing rapidly. **Il** will then place a piece **de papier sur la table. Vous** will pay **le**

garçon ou perhaps **vous** will pay **à la caisse.**
(kess)
cashier

> **Excusez-moi.**
> **L'addition, s'il**
> **vous plaît.**

> **Bien sûr,**
> **Monsieur.**

> **Un dîner**
> **excellent. Merci.**

> **Il n'y a pas de**
> **quoi.* Au revoir.**

If your bill or the menu is marked **"service compris,"** then your tip has already been included in
(sair-vees) *(koh⁽ⁿ⁾-pree)*
included

your bill. If the service is not included in **l'addition,** round the bill up **ou** simply leave what you

consider an appropriate amount for your **garçon sur la table.** When **vous** dine out on your

voyage, it is always a good idea to make a reservation. It can be difficult to get into a popular
(vwah-yahzh)
trip
(reh-stoh-rah⁽ⁿ⁾)
restaurant. Nevertheless, the experience is well worth the trouble **vous** might encounter to

obtain a reservation. **Et** remember, **vous savez** enough **français** to make a reservation. Just
(sah-vay)
know

speak slowly and clearly. This is a good phrase to know:

(eel) *(nyah)* *(pah)* *(kwah)*
*Il n'y a pas de quoi.
it is nothing/you're welcome

☐ **le sport** *(spor)*	sport		_____
☐ **stopper** *(stoh-pay)*	to stop		_____
☐ **stupide** *(stew-peed)*	stupid	**S**	_____
☐ **la Suède** *(swed)*	Sweden		_____
☐ **la Suisse** *(swees)*	Switzerland		_____

Remember these key **mots** when dining out **à la française.** *(frah(n)-sez)*
in the French manner

(sair-vur) *(gar-soh(n))*
le serveur/le garçon _____
waiter

(sair-vuz)
la serveuse _____
waitress

(lah-dee-syoh(n))
l'addition _____ *l'addition, l'addition*
bill

(poor-bwahr)
le pourboire _____
tip

(muh-new) *(kart)*
le menu/ la carte _____
menu

(eel)(nyah) *(pah)* *(duh)(kwah)*
il n'y a pas de quoi _____
it's nothing/you're welcome

(ek-skew-zay-mwah)
excusez-moi _____
excuse me

(mair-see)
merci _____
thank you

(seel) *(voo)* *(play)*
s'il vous plaît _____
please

(doh(n)-nay-mwah)
donnez-moi . . . _____
give me

Voilà une sample **conversation** *(koh(n)-vair-sah-syoh(n))* involving paying **la facture** *(fahk-tewr)* when leaving **un hôtel.**
bill

Jeannette:	**Excusez-moi. Je voudrais payer la facture.** *(voo-dray)* *(pay-yay)* to pay
	Excusez-moi. Je voudrais payer la facture.
L'Hôtelier: *(loh-tel-yay)* hotelkeeper	**Quelle chambre, s'il vous plaît?** *(kel)* which room
	_____
Jeannette:	**Numéro trois cent dix.** *(noo-may-roh)* number
	_____
L'Hôtelier:	**Merci. Une minute, s'il vous plaît.**
	_____
L'Hôtelier:	**Voilà la facture.**
	_____

If **vous** have any problems **avec les nombres,** just ask someone to write out **la somme,** *(sohm)* so that
sum

vous can be sure you understand everything correctly,

"S'il vous plaît, écrivez- moi la somme. Merci." *(ay-kree-vay-mwah)*
please write for me

Practice: _____
(Please write the sum for me. Thank you.)

- ☐ **supérieur** *(syoo-pay-ree-ur)* . . . . superior, upper _____
- ☐ **la surprise** *(sewr-preez)* . . . . surprise _____
- ☐ **sympathique** *(sa(n)-pah-teek)* . . . . likeable, nice   **S** _____
-    **– Qu'il est sympa!** *(keel)(ay)(sa(n)-pah)* . . . . Oh, he's so nice. _____
- ☐ **le système** *(see-stem)* . . . . system _____

Maintenant, let's take a break from **les additions et l'argent** *(lar-zhah(n))* **et** learn some fun **nouveaux**
money new

mots. Vous can always practice these **mots** by using your flash cards at the back of this **livre.**

Carry these flash cards in your purse, pocket, briefcase **ou** knapsack **et** *use them!*

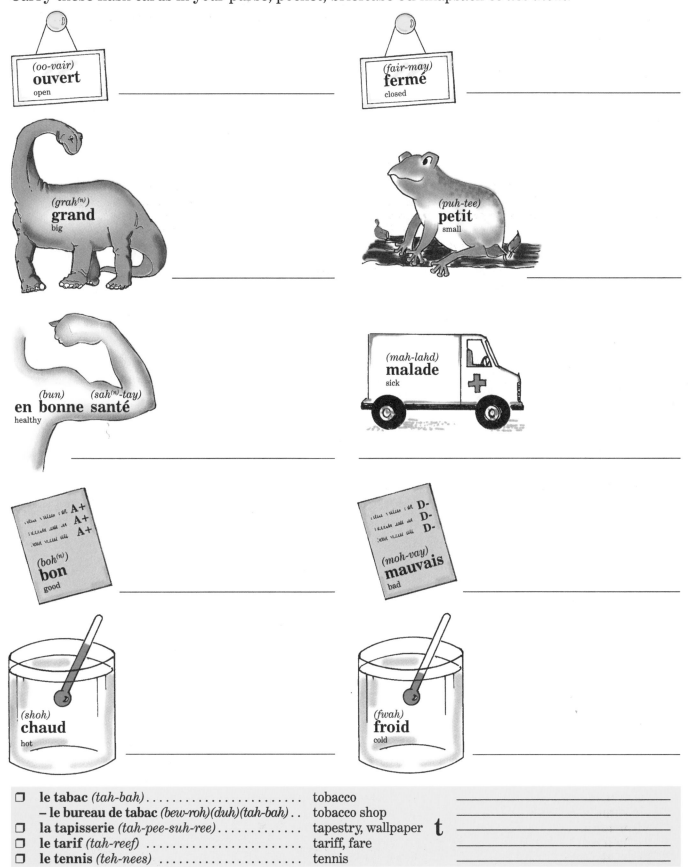

(oo-vair)
ouvert
open

_____

(fair-may)
fermé
closed

_____

(grah(n))
grand
big

_____

(puh-tee)
petit
small

_____

(bun) (sah(n)-tay)
en bonne santé
healthy

_____

(mah-lahd)
malade
sick

_____

(boh(n))
bon
good

_____

(moh-vay)
mauvais
bad

_____

(shoh)
chaud
hot

_____

(fwah)
froid
cold

_____

☐ **le tabac** *(tah-bah)*	tobacco	
– **le bureau de tabac** *(bew-roh)(duh)(tah-bah)* . .	tobacco shop	**t** _____
☐ **la tapisserie** *(tah-pee-suh-ree)*	tapestry, wallpaper	_____
☐ **le tarif** *(tah-reef)*	tariff, fare	_____
☐ **le tennis** *(teh-nees)*	tennis	_____

71

(koor)
court _____
short

(lohng)
long _____
long

25

120

(lah(n))
lent _____
slow

(rah-peed)
rapide _____
fast

(grah(n)) (oh)
grand/haut _____
tall   high

(puh-tee) (bah)
petit/ bas _____
short   low

(vee-yuh)
vieux _____
old

(zhun)
jeune _____
young

(shair)
cher _____
expensive

(boh(n)) (mar-shay)
bon marché _____
inexpensive

(reesh)
riche _____
rich

(poh-vruh)
pauvre _____
poor

(boh-koo)
beaucoup _____
a lot

(puh)
un peu _____
a little

❏   **la terrasse** *(tay-rahs)* . . . .   terrace, sidewalk cafe _____
❏   **thermal** *(tair-mahl)* . . . .   thermal _____
   – les eaux thermales *(lay)(zoh)(tair-mahl)* . .   hot springs   **t** _____
❏   **le théâtre** *(tay-ah-truh)* . . . .   theater _____
❏   **le ticket** *(tee-kay)* . . . .   ticket _____

Voilà de nouveaux verbes.
some

(sah-vwahr)
savoir _____
to know (fact, address)

(leer)
lire _____
to read

(poo-vwahr)
pouvoir _____
to be able to, can

(duh-vwahr)
devoir _____
to have to, must, to owe

Study the patterns below closely, as **vous** will use these verbs a lot.

(sah-vwahr)
savoir
to know

Je _sais/_ _____ **tout.**
everything

Vous _savez/_ _____ **parler français.**
to speak

Il _sait/_ _____ **parler français.**
Elle
to speak

Nous _savons/_ _____ **parler anglais.**

Ils ne _savent/_ _____ **pas parler français.**
Elles

(poo-vwahr)
pouvoir
to be able to, can

Je _peux/_ _____ **commander un café.**

(ah-shuh-tay)
Vous _pouvez/_ _____ **acheter un journal.**

(ah(n)-vwah-yay)
Il _peut/_ _____ **envoyer une lettre.**
Elle
read

(mah(n)-zhay)
Nous _pouvons/_ _____ **manger au restaurant.**

(pay-yay) *(fahk-tewr)*
Ils _peuvent/_ _____ **payer la facture.**
Elles
bill (hotel)

(leer)
lire
to read

Je _lis/_ _____ **le livre.**

(ruh-vew)
Vous _lisez/_ _____ **la revue.**
magazine

Il _lit/_ _____ **le menu.**
Elle

Nous _lisons/_ _____ **beaucoup.**
a lot

(zhoor-nahl)
Ils _lisent/_ _____ **le journal.**
Elles
newspaper

(duh-vwahr)
devoir
to have to, must, to owe

(ah-prah(n)-druh)
Je _dois/_ _____ **apprendre le français.**

(leer)
Vous _devez/_ _____ **lire le livre.**

(reh-stay)
Il _doit/_ _____ **rester à l'hôtel.**
Elle
remain

(vee-zee-tay)
Nous _devons/_ _____ **visiter Paris.**
visit

(pay-yay)
Ils _doivent/_ _____ **payer l'addition.**
Elles
bill (restaurant)

❑ **la tour** *(tour)* .... tower _____
❑ **le tour** *(tour)* .... circumference, tour _____
– **Le Tour de France** .... bicycle race in France **t** _____
❑ **tricolore** *(tree-koh-lor)* .... tricolored _____
– **le drapeau tricolore** *(drah-poh)* .. French flag (**bleu, blanc, rouge**) _____

Notice that "**pouvoir**," "**devoir**," et "**savoir**" along with "**voudrais**" and "**voudrions**" can be combined

with another verb.

(say) **Je sais trouver l'adresse.** know how to find *(say)* *(koh⁽ⁿ⁾-mah⁽ⁿ⁾-day)* **Je sais commander une bière.** to order	*(poo-voh⁽ⁿ⁾)* *(reh-stay)* **Nous pouvons rester à Paris.** can *(ah⁽ⁿ⁾-vwah-yay)* *(let-ruh)* **Nous pouvons envoyer une lettre.**	*(dwah)* **Elle doit dormir.** must/has to sleep **Elle doit payer l'addition.**

(say) *(par-lay)*
Je sais parler français.
I know how
(puh)
Je peux commander un livre.
can
(dwah)
Je dois parler français.
must
(voo-dray)
Je voudrais parler français.
would like

(poo-vay-voo)
Pouvez-vous translate the sentences **en français? Les réponses sont en bas.**
can

1. I know how to speak French. _____

2. They can pay the restaurant bill. _____

3. He has to pay the hotel bill. _____

4. We know how to speak English. _____

5. She knows how to speak French. _____

6. We know how to read French. _____

7. I cannot find the hotel. _____

8. We are not able to (cannot) understand French. _____

9. I would like to visit Lyon. _____

10. She reads the newspaper. _____

Maintenant, draw **des lignes** *(leen-yuh)* **entre** the opposites **en bas.** Do not forget to say them out loud.

Say **ces mots** *(say)* every day to describe **les choses dans votre** *(voh-truh)* **maison, dans votre** **école ou dans** *(ay-kohl)*

votre bureau.

(grah(n)) **grand**

(gohsh) **gauche**

(zhun) **jeune**

(poh-vruh) **pauvre**

malade

long

beaucoup

(boh(n)) **bon**

(shoh) **chaud**

(bah) **en bas**

lent

(shair) **cher**

(fair-may) **fermé**

(oh) **en haut**

(oo-vair) **ouvert**

(koor) **court**

(mar-shay) **bon marché**

(puh) **un peu**

(bun) **en bonne santé**

rapide

(vee-yuh) **vieux**

(puh-tee) **petit**

(dwaht) **droite**

(fwah) **froid**

riche

(moh-vay) **mauvais**

❑ **unique** *(ew-neek)*	sole, only, single	_____
– **l'enfant unique** *(lah(n)-fah(n))(tew-neek)*	only child	_____
❑ **universel** *(ew-nee-vair-sel)*	universal	**u** _____
❑ **l'université** *(lew-nee-vair-see-tay)*	university	_____
❑ **l'urgence** *(lewr-zhah(n)s)*	urgency, emergency	_____

19   *(vwah-yah-zhur)*   *(vwah-yahzh)*
Le Voyageur Voyage
traveler   travels

(ee-air)
Hier à Bordeaux!
yesterday

(oh-zhoor-dwee)
Aujourd'hui à Tours!
today

(duh-ma^{n})
Demain à Nice!
tomorrow

If you know a few key **mots,** traveling can be easy in most French-speaking countries. **La**

(nay) (pah)
France n'est pas très grande, in fact, it is slightly smaller than the state of Texas. **Donc, c'est** *(doh^{n}k)*
is not   therefore

(fah-seel)
très facile de voyager in France. **Comment voyagez-vous en France?**
easy

(vwah-yahzh)
Etienne voyage en auto.
travels   car

Marie-Anne voyage en bateau.
boat

Xavier voyage en moto.

Colette voyage en train.

Françoise voyage en avion.
airplane

Lucette voyage en autobus.

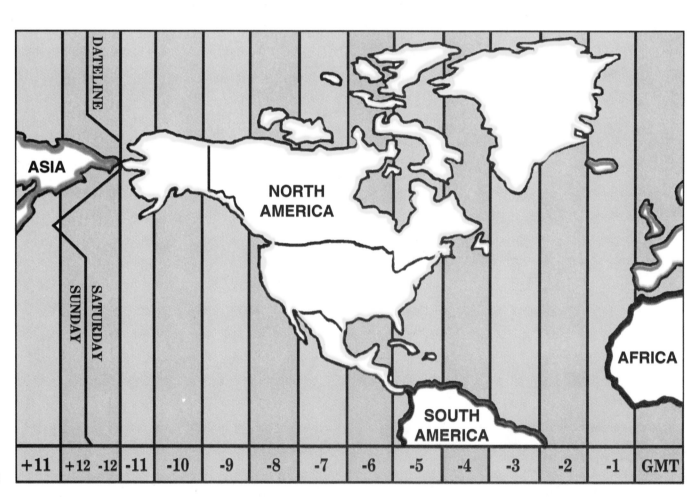

+11	+12	-12	-11	-10	-9	-8	-7	-6	-5	-4	-3	-2	-1	GMT

Quand vous are traveling, **vous** will want to tell others your nationality **et vous** will meet

people from all corners of the world. Can you guess where people are from if they say one of

the following? **Les réponses** are in your glossary beginning on page 108.

(vya⁽ⁿ⁾) *(dah⁽ⁿ⁾-gluh-tair)*
Je viens d'Angleterre. _____
come   from

(dee-tah-lee)
Je viens d'Italie. _____

(day) (zay-tah-zoo-nee)
Je viens des États-Unis. _____

(deh-spahn-yuh)
Je viens d'Espagne. _____

(bel-zheek)
Je viens de Belgique. _____

(swees)
Je viens de Suisse. _____

(mah-rohk)
Je viens du Maroc. _____

(day-kohs)
Je viens d'Ecosse. _____

(doh-treesh)
Je viens d'Autriche. _____

(noo) *(vuh-noh⁽ⁿ⁾)* *(roo-see)*
Nous venons de Russie. _____
we   come

(dahl-mahn-yuh)
Nous venons d'Allemagne. _____

(dees-rah-el)
Nous venons d'Israël. _____

(tew-nee-zee)
Nous venons de Tunisie. _____

(dahl-zhay-ree)
Il vient d'Algérie. _____
he   comes

(deer-lahnd)
Il vient d'Irelande. _____

(por-too-gahl)
Elle vient du Portugal. _____
she   comes

(dah-freek)
Elle vient d'Afrique du Sud. _____

Je viens du Canada. _____

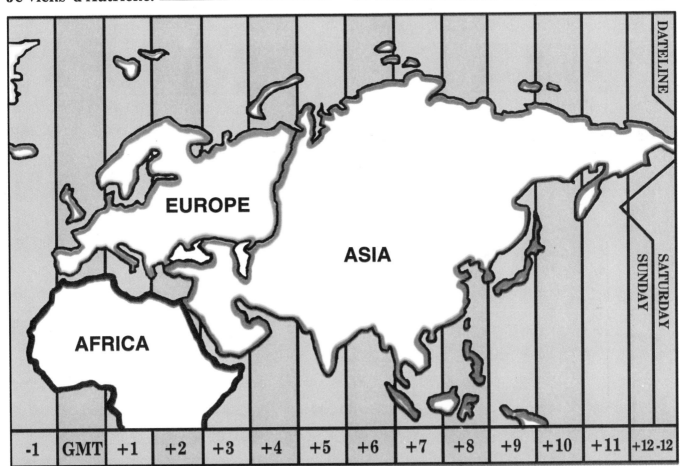

Le mot for "trip" is taken from **le mot "voyager,"** *(vwah-yah-zhay)* / to travel / which makes it easy: **voyage.** *(vwah-yahzh)* / trip / **Beaucoup de**

mots revolve around the concept of travel which is exactly what **vous voudriez faire.** Practice

the following **mots** many times. **Vous** will see them often.

(vwah-yah-zhay)
voyager_____
to travel

(vwah-yah-zhur)
le voyageur_____
traveler

(ah-zhah(n)s) *(vwah-yahzh)*
une agence de voyage_____ _____
travel agency

(boh(n))
Bon voyage!_____
have a good trip

If **vous** choose **aller en auto,** *(ah-lay)* / to go / **voilà** a few key **mots.**

(loh-toh-root)
l'autoroute_____
freeway

(root)
la route_____
road

(koh(n)-trah-vah(n)-syoh(n))
une contravention_____
parking ticket

(vwah-tewr) *(loh-kah-syoh(n))*
une voiture de location_____
rental car

(ah-zhah(n)s) *(loh-kah-syoh(n))* *(vwah-tewr)*
une agence de location de voitures_____
car-rental agency

(stah-syoh(n)) *(day-sah(n)s)*
la station d'essence_____
service station

En bas **il y a** *(eel-yah)* / there are / some basic signs which **vous** should **aussi** *(oh-see)* learn to recognize quickly.

(ah(n)-tray)
entrer_____
to enter

(sor-teer)
sortir_____
to exit

ENTRÉE

SORTIE

(lah(n)-tray)
l'entrée_____
entrance

(pra(n)-see-pahl)
l'entrée principale_____
main

(sor-tee)
la sortie_____
exit

(suh-koor)
la sortie de secours_____
emergency exit

POUSSEZ

TIREZ

(poo-say)
poussez_____
push (doors)

(tee-ray)
tirez_____
pull (doors)

❑ **les vacances** *(vah-kah(n)s)* . . . . vacation, holidays   _____
 – **les grandes vacances** . . . . summer vacation   _____
❑ **la valse** *(vahls)* . . . . waltz   _____
❑ **la vanille** *(vah-nee-yuh)* . . . . vanilla   **V**   _____
 – **la glace à la vanille** *(glahs)* . . . . vanilla ice cream   _____

78

Let's learn the basic travel verbs. Take out a piece of paper **et** make up your own sentences

with these **nouveaux mots.** Follow the same pattern **vous** have in previous Steps.

(prah⁽ⁿ⁾-druh) (lah-vyoh⁽ⁿ⁾)
prendre l'avion _____
to fly, to take the plane

(ah-ree-vay)
arriver _____
to arrive

(sor-teer)
sortir _____
to leave, to go out

(eel-yah)
il y a _____
there is, there are

(ah-lay)
aller _____
to go

(par-teer)
partir _____
to depart, to leave

(fair) (vah-leez)
faire les valises _____
to pack

(shah⁽ⁿ⁾-zhay) (tra⁽ⁿ⁾)
changer de train _____
to transfer (trains)

Voilà de nouveaux mots pour votre voyage.
some

(lah-ay-roh-por)
l'aéroport _____
airport

(kay)
le quai _____
platform

(loh-rair)
l'horaire _____
timetable

DE PARIS À TOURS		
Départ	**Nº de train**	**Arrivée**
00:41	50	09:41
07:40	19	16:40
12:15	22	21:15
14:32	10	23:32
21:40	04	06:40

(gar)
la gare _____
train station

Avec ces **mots, vous êtes** ready for any **voyage**, anywhere. **Vous** should have no **problèmes avec**
these   (voo) (zet)

these verbs, just remember the basic "plug-in" formula **vous** have already learned. Use that

knowledge to translate the following thoughts **en français. Les réponses sont en bas.**
                                                                              into

1.   I fly to Paris. _____

2.   I transfer trains in Toulon. _____

3.   He goes to Marseille. _____ Il va à Marseille. Il va à Marseille. _____

4.   We arrive tomorrow. _____

5.   We buy three tickets to Tours. _____

6.   They travel to Strasbourg. _____

7.   Where is the train to Bordeaux? _____

8.   How can we travel to Switzerland? With Swiss Air or with Air France? _____
_____

Voilà some **mots importants pour le voyageur.**
                                                  traveler

DE PARIS À TOURS		
Départ	Nº de train	Arrivée
00:41	50	09:41
07:40	19	16:40
12:15	22	21:15
14:32	10	23:32
21:40	04	06:40

(oh-kew-pay)
occupé _____
occupied

(lee-bruh)
libre _____
free

(koh⁽ⁿ⁾-par-tuh-mah⁽ⁿ⁾)
le compartiment _____
compartment, wagon

(plahs)
la place _____
seat

(day-par)
le départ _____
departure

(lah-ree-vay)
l'arrivée _____
arrival

(ay-trah⁽ⁿ⁾-zhay)
étranger / international _____
abroad

(a⁽ⁿ⁾-tay-ree-ur)
intérieur _____
domestic, internal

Increase your travel **mots** by writing out **les mots en bas et** practicing the sample **phrases** *(frahz)* out loud. Practice asking **questions avec "où."** It will help you later.

(poor)
pour _____
for

Où est le train pour Paris?

(port)
la porte _____
gate

Où est la porte numéro 5?

(day) (zohb-zhay)(troo-vay)
le bureau des objets trouvés _____
lost-and-found office

Y a-t-il un bureau des objets trouvés?

(por-tur)
le porteur _____
porter

Où est le porteur? Où est le porteur?

Où est le porteur?

(vohl)
le vol _____
flight

Où est le vol pour Marseille?

(koh⁽ⁿ⁾-seen-yuh)
la consigne _____
left-luggage office

Y a-t-il une consigne?

(bew-roh)   (shah⁽ⁿ⁾zh)
le bureau de change _____
money-exchange office

Où est le bureau de change?

(ghee-shay)
le guichet _____
counter

Où est le guichet numéro sept?

(sahl)   (dah-tah⁽ⁿ⁾t)
la salle d'attente _____
waiting room

Y a-t-il une salle d'attente?

(vah-goh⁽ⁿ⁾-reh-stoh-rah⁽ⁿ⁾)
le wagon-restaurant _____
dining car

Y a-t-il un wagon-restaurant dans le train?

(vah-goh⁽ⁿ⁾-lee)
le wagon-lit _____
sleeping car

Y a-t-il un wagon-lit dans le train?

(koo-shet)
la couchette _____
berth, bunk

Y a-t-il des couchettes dans le train?

_____ (when) _____ (when) *(par)* **part le train?**

_____ (what) _____ (what) *(key) (suh)(pahs)* **est-ce qui se passe?** is happening

❏ **la vierge** *(vee-airzh)*	virgin	
– **la Sainte Vierge** *(sa⁽ⁿ⁾t)(vee-airzh)*	Virgin Mary	**V**
❏ **la vigne** *(veen-yuh)*	grape vine	
❏ **le vigneron** *(veen-yur-oh⁽ⁿ⁾)*	wine-grower	
❏ **le vignoble** *(veen-yoh-bluh)*	vineyard	

81

Pouvez-vous lire les phrases suivantes?
can .... read .... *(frahz)* ..... following

(voo) *(zet)* *(ah-see)*
Vous êtes maintenant assis dans l'avion
seated

et vous voyagez en France. Vous avez *(voo)* *(zah-vay)*

de l'argent, votre billet, votre passeport

(voh) *(vah-leez)*
et vos valises. Vous êtes maintenant
your .. suitcases

touriste. Vous arrivez demain à 14:15 en

France. Bon voyage! Amusez-vous

(bya(n))
bien.
well

(eel-yah) *(lohm-nee-boos)* *(loh-toh-rye)* *(lah(n))* *(rah-peed)*
En France il y a many different types of trains – **l'omnibus et l'autorail sont lents; le rapide**
.... there are

(lek-spress)
et l'express are much faster. If **vous** plan to travel a long distance, **vous** may wish to catch an

Inter-City train or **TGV** (**t**rain **à** **g**rande **v**itesse) which travels faster **et** makes fewer

intermediate stops.

☐	**le village** *(vee-lahzh)*	village		_____
☐	**le vin** *(va(n))*	wine		_____
☐	**la visite** *(vee-zeet)*	visit	**v**	_____
☐	**la vitamine** *(vee-tah-meen)*	vitamin		_____
☐	**le vocabulaire** *(voh-kah-bew-lair)*	vocabulary		_____

Knowing these travel **mots** will make your holiday twice as enjoyable **et** at least three times as easy. Review these **mots** by doing the crossword puzzle **en bas**. Drill yourself on this Step by selecting other destinations **et** ask your own **questions** about **les trains, les autobus et les avions** that go there. Select more **nouveaux mots de votre dictionnaire et** ask your own questions beginning with **quand, où et combien**. **Les réponses** to the crossword puzzle are at the bottom of the next page.

ACROSS

1. money
2. train station
3. timetable
4. to pay
5. occupied
6. counter, window
7. we
8. with
9. lost-and-found office
10. no
11. airport
12. free (unoccupied)
13. to go
14. passport
15. entrance

DOWN

1. to arrive
2. thank you
3. to change trains
4. waiting room
5. traveler
6. dining car
7. have a good trip
8. platform
9. to know
11. she
12. to leave, to go out
13. weather, time
14. seat
15. exit
16. nothing

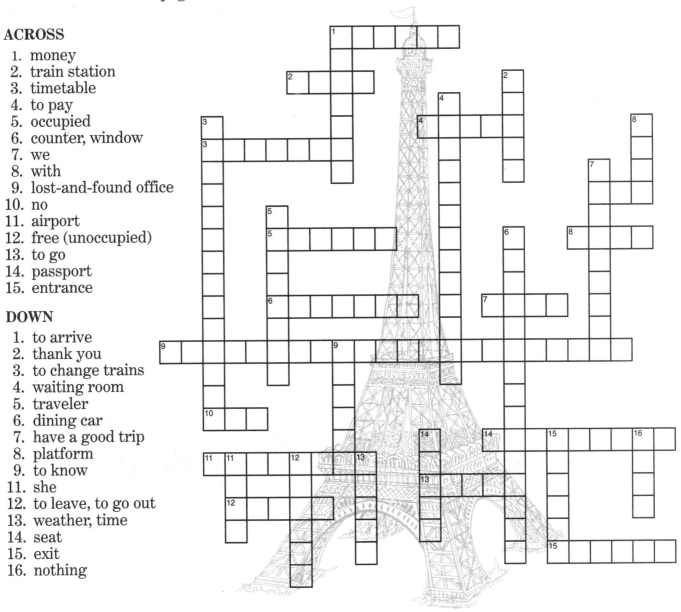

Eiffel Tower – La Tour Eiffel is Paris' most famous landmark. It was first opened in 1889 and soars to a height of over 1,000 feet.

Most "w" words are foreign additions to **le français**.

- ☐ **le wagon** *(vah-goh⁽ⁿ⁾)* . . . . railroad car
- ☐ **le week-end** *(week-end)* . . . . weekend
- ☐ **le western** *(wes-tairn)* . . . . western (film)
- ☐ **le whisky** *(wee-skee)* . . . . whisky

W

_____
_____
_____
_____

What about inquiring about **le tarif** *(tah-reef)* **des billets?** *(bee-ay)* **Vous pouvez** ask these **questions.**
price   tickets

Combien coûte un billet pour Lille? *(kohm-bya⁽ⁿ⁾)* *(leel)* _____

Combien coûte un billet pour Bayonne? *(by-ohn)* _____

Combien coûte un billet pour Bordeaux? _____

un aller simple *(ah-lay)* *(sa⁽ⁿ⁾-pluh)* _____
one-way ticket

un aller-retour *(ah-lay-ruh-tour)* _____
round-trip ticket

What about times of **départs et arrivées?** *(day-par)* *(ah-ree-vay)* **Vous pouvez** ask **ces questions aussi.**
departure   arrival

À quelle heure part l'avion pour Lyon? *(kel)* *(uhr)* *(lee-oh⁽ⁿ⁾)* _____
at what   time   leaves   for

À quelle heure part le train pour Londres? *(loh⁽ⁿ⁾-druh)* _____

À quelle heure arrive l'avion de New York? *(ah-reev)* _____
arrives   from

À quelle heure arrive le train de Grenoble? *(gruh-noh-bluh)* _____

À quelle heure part l'avion pour Nice? *(nees)* _____

Vous have just arrived **en France. Vous êtes à la gare. Où voudriez-vous aller? À Limoges?** *(voo-dree-ay-voo)*
at   would you like

À Strasbourg? Tell that to the person at the **guichet** selling **les billets!** *(ghee-shay)*
window

Je voudrais aller à Rennes. *(ren)* _____
go

À quelle heure part le train pour Rennes? *(kel)* _____

Combien coûte un billet pour Rennes? *(koot)* _____

84

Maintenant that **vous** know the words essential for traveling **en France ou en Suisse**, what are some speciality items **vous** might go in search of?

(froh-mahzh)
le fromage
cheese

(soo-vuh-neer)
les souvenirs
souvenirs

(shoh-koh-laht)
des chocolats
chocolates

(vet-mah⁽ⁿ⁾)
les vêtements
clothes

(par-fuh⁽ⁿ⁾)
le parfum
perfume

(tah-bloh)
les tableaux
pictures

Consider using FRENCH *a language map*® as well. FRENCH *a language map*® is the perfect companion for your travels when **vous** may not wish to take along this **livre**. Each section focuses on essentials for your **voyage**. Your *Language Map*® is not meant to replace learning **français**, but will help you in the event **vous** forget something and need a little bit of help. For more information about the *Language Map*® Series, please turn to page 132.

❐ **le zèbre** *(zeh-bruh)*	zebra		
– zébré *(zay-bray)*	striped		
❐ **le zèle** *(zel)*	zeal, ardor	**Z**	
– zélé *(zay-lay)*	zealous		
❐ **le zénith** *(zay-neet)*	zenith, peak		

20   La Carte ou Le Menu
(kart)   *(muh-new)*

menu

Vous êtes maintenant en France et vous avez une chambre. Vous avez faim. Où y a-t-il
(fa⁽ⁿ⁾)   *(yah-teel)*

have   hunger   is there

un bon restaurant? First of all, **il y a** different types of places to eat. Let's learn them.
(eel-yah)

there are

---

le restaurant
(reh-stoh-rah⁽ⁿ⁾)

exactly what it says with a variety of meals and prices

la brasserie
(brah-suh-ree)

originally a beer salon, but now also a restaurant

l'auberge
(loh-bairzh)

originally a country inn, but it can be an inviting city restaurant as well

le bistro
(bee-stroh)

slang for **le bar** or a small, intimate restaurant with lots of atmosphere

le bar
(bar)

serves morning pastries, but concentrates on liquid refreshments

---

If **vous** look around you **dans un restaurant français, vous** will see that some **coutumes**
(koo-tewn)

customs

françaises might be different from yours. Sharing **tables avec** others **est** a common **et très**

pleasant custom. Before beginning **votre repas,** be sure to wish those sharing your table –
(ruh-pah)

meal

"**Bon appétit!**" Your turn to practice now.
(boh⁽ⁿ⁾) (nah-pay-tee)

enjoy your meal

_____

(enjoy your meal)

And at least one more time for practice!

_____

(enjoy your meal)

Start imagining now all the new taste treats you will experience abroad. Try all of the different

types of eating establishments mentioned on the previous page. Experiment. If **vous trouvez**

un restaurant that **vous voudriez** to try, consider calling ahead to make a **réservation**. *(ray-zair-vah-syoh⁽ⁿ⁾)*

<u>**"Je voudrais faire une réservation."**</u> If **vous avez besoin d'un menu**, catch the attention of **le**
   I   would like

serveur, saying,

> **"Monsieur! Le menu, s'il vous plaît."**

_____
               (Sir! The menu, please.)

If your **serveur** asks if **vous** enjoyed your

repas, a smile **et** a **"Oui, merci,"** will tell him

that you did.

Most **restaurants français** post **le menu** outside **ou** inside. Do not hesitate to ask to see **la carte**

before being seated so **vous** know what type of **repas et** *(pree)* **prix vous** will encounter. Most
                                            meals   prices

restaurants offer **un plat du jour ou un menu à prix fixe**. These are complete **repas** at a fair
                 daily special   price fixed   meals

(pree)
prix.
price

❑ **la zone** *(zohn)*	zone	_____
– **une zone de silence** *(see-lah⁽ⁿ⁾s)*	quiet zone	_____
❑ **le zoo** *(zoh)*	zoo **Z**	_____
– **un jardin zoologique** *(zhar-da⁽ⁿ⁾)*	zoological garden	_____
❑ **Zut!** *(zewt)*	Darn! Rats!	_____

En France, *(eel-yah)* **il y a** *(ruh-pah)* **trois** main **repas** to enjoy every day, plus perhaps **un café et une pâtisserie** *(pah-tee-suh-ree)*

there are

pour le voyageur fatigué late in **l'après-midi.**

(puh-tee-day-zhuh-nay)

le petit-déjeuner _____
breakfast
        This meal usually consists of **café ou thé**, croissants, butter and marmalade.

        Check serving times before **vous** retire for the night or you might miss out!

(day-zhuh-nay)

le déjeuner _____
mid-day meal
        generally served from 12:00 to 14:00; you will be able to find any type

        of meal, **grand ou petit**, served at this time.

(dee-nay)

le dîner _____
evening meal
        generally served from 19:30 to 22:00. This meal is meant to be relished,

        surrounded by good friends and a pleasant atmosphere.

Maintenant for a preview of delights to come . . . At the back of this **livre, vous** will find a sample

menu français. *(lee-zay)* **Lisez le menu aujourd'hui et** *(ah-pruh-nay)* **apprenez les** *(noo-voh)* **nouveaux mots.** When **vous** are
        read   today   learn

ready to leave on your **voyage**, cut out **le menu**, fold it, **et** carry it in your pocket, wallet **ou** purse.

Before you go, how do **vous** say these **trois** phrases which are so very important for the hungry

traveler?

Excuse me. I would like to make a reservation. _____

Waiter! The menu, please. _____

Enjoy your meal! _____

_____ *(mah⁽ⁿ⁾zh)* **mange des escargots?** _____ *(bwah)* **boit du thé?**
(who)   eats   (who)   drinks

(who)

_____ **voyage à** *(kay-bek)* **Québec?**
(who)

Learning the following should help you to identify what kind of meat **vous** have ordered **et comment** it will be prepared.

- ❏ **boeuf** *(buf)* . . . . beef _____
- ❏ **veau** *(voh)* . . . . veal _____
- ❏ **porc** *(por)* . . . . pork _____
- ❏ **mouton** *(moo-toh⁽ⁿ⁾)* . . . . mutton

La carte below has the main categories **vous** will find in most restaurants. Learn them

aujourd'hui so that **vous** will easily recognize them when you dine **à Paris ou à Nice.** Be sure

to write the words in the blanks below.

(muh-new)
Menu

(or-duh-vruh)
le hors-d'oeuvre
appetizers

_____

(poh-tahzh)
le potage
soups

_____

(uh)
les oeufs
eggs

_____

(voh-lie)
la volaille
poultry

_____

(lay-gewm)
les légumes
vegetables

_____

(pwah-soh⁽ⁿ⁾)
les poissons
fish and seafood dishes

_____

(vee-ah⁽ⁿ⁾d)
les viandes
meat dishes

_____

(sah-lahd)
les salades
salads

_____

(day-sair)
les desserts
desserts

_____

(kahs-kroot)
le casse-croûte
snacks

_____

(fwee)
les fruits
fruit
(froh-mahzh)
ou les fromages
cheese

_____

(pah-tee-suh-ree)
les pâtisseries
pastries

_____

(bwah-soh⁽ⁿ⁾)
les boissons
beverages

_____

❏ **volaille** *(voh-lie)*	poultry	_____
❏ **agneau** *(ahn-yoh)*	lamb	_____
❏ **gibier** *(zhee-bee-ay)*	game	_____
❏ **frit** *(free)*	fried	_____
❏ **rôti** *(roh-tee)*	roasted	_____

Vous may also order **légumes** *(lay-gewn)* **avec votre repas** *(ruh-pah)* **ou** perhaps **une salade verte** *(vairt)*. One day at an open-air **marché** *(mar-shay)* will teach you **les noms** for all the different kinds of **légumes et fruits** *(fwee)*, plus it will be a delightful experience for you. **Vous pouvez** always consult your menu guide at the back of **ce** *(suh)* **livre** if **vous** *(voo)* **oubliez** *(zoo-blee-ay)* **le nom correct**. **Maintenant vous** are seated **et le serveur arrive** *(ah-reev)*.

vegetables / meal / green / market / fuit / can / this / forget / waiter

La carte, s'il vous plaît.

Et comme boisson?

Un verre de vin blanc, s'il vous plaît.

Le petit-déjeuner *(puh-tee-day-zhuh-nay)* **est un peu** *(puh)* **différent** *(dee-fay-rah⁽ⁿ⁾)* because **il est** fairly standardized **et vous** will frequently take it at **votre hôtel**, as **il est généralement** *(zhay-nay-rahl-mah⁽ⁿ⁾)* included in **le prix de votre chambre**.

breakfast / little

En bas il y a des exemples of what **vous pouvez** expect to greet you **le matin**.

Boissons

café

café au lait

thé

chocolat

jus d'orange
juice

jus de tomate

jus de pomme
apple

lait

et . . .

pain

croissants

jambon
ham

confiture
jam

beurre

oeuf à la coque
soft-boiled

oeufs brouillés
scrambled

omelette nature

☐ **cuit** *(kwee)*	cooked	_____
☐ **cuit au four** *(kwee)(toh)(foor)*	baked	_____
☐ **grillé** *(gree-ay)*	grilled	_____
☐ **farci** *(far-see)*	stuffed	_____
☐ **fumé** *(few-may)*	smoked	_____

Voilà an example of what **vous** might select for your evening meal. Using your menu guide on pages 117 and 118, as well as what **vous** have learned in this Step, fill in the blanks *in English* with what **vous** believe your **serveur** will bring you. **Les réponses sont** below.

Hors-d'oeuvre
Oeufs durs mayonnaise

_____

Salade
Salade niçoise avec du pain frais

_____

Entrée
Côtes d'agneau grillées à la menthe et au vinaigre

_____

Dessert
Mousse au chocolat

_____

(when)   (how)   (why)

LES RÉPONSES

Appetizer: Hard-boiled eggs with mayonnaise
Salad: Mixed salad with tuna, string beans and potatoes
Entree: Grilled lamb chops with mint sauce
Dessert: Chocolate mousse

91

Maintenant est a good time for a quick review. Draw lines between **les mots français et** their English equivalents.

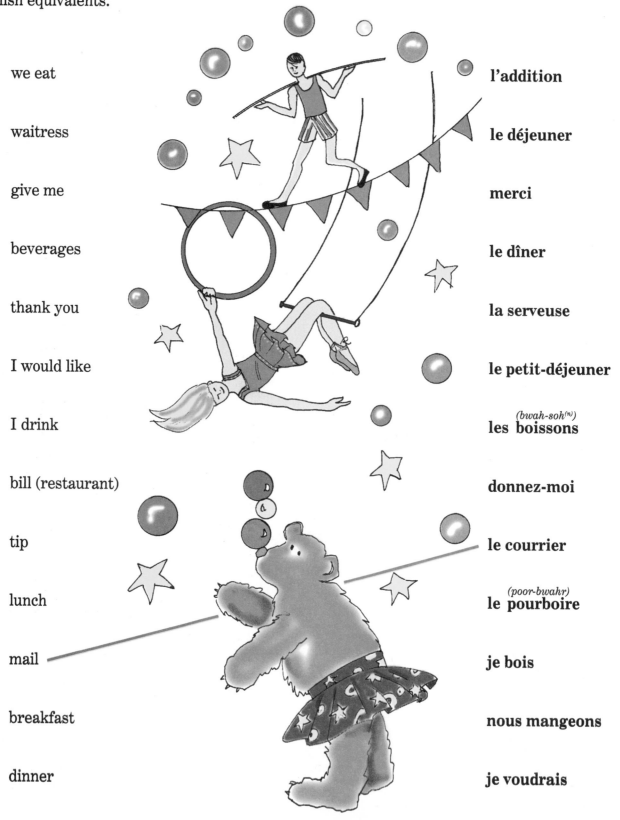

we eat   **l'addition**

waitress   **le déjeuner**

give me   **merci**

beverages   **le dîner**

thank you   **la serveuse**

I would like   **le petit-déjeuner**

I drink   *(bwah-soh[n])* **les boissons**

bill (restaurant)   **donnez-moi**

tip   **le courrier**

lunch   *(poor-bwahr)* **le pourboire**

mail   **je bois**

breakfast   **nous mangeons**

dinner   **je voudrais**

Voilà a few holidays which you might experience during your visit.
- ❑ **Nouvel An** *(noo-vel)(ah[n])* .... New Year's Day
- ❑ **Noël** *(noh-el)* .... Christmas
- ❑ **Vendredi-Saint** *(vah[n]-druh-dee-sa[n]t)* .... Good Friday
- ❑ **Pâques** *(pah-kuh)* .... Easter

(kess) *(key)*
Qu'est-ce qui est différent about **le téléphone en France?** Well, **vous** never notice such things
what

until **vous** want to use them. **Les téléphones** allow you to call **des amis**, reserve **les billets de**
(day) *(zah-mee)*
friends   tickets

théâtre, de concert ou de ballet, make emergency calls, check on the hours of a **musée**, rent
(bah-leh)   *(mew-zay)*

une voiture et all those other **choses** which **nous faisons** on a daily basis. It also gives you a
do

certain amount of **liberté quand vous pouvez** make your own **appels de téléphone**.
(ah-pel)
calls

Les téléphones can usually be found

everywhere: in the **bureaux de poste**, on the
post offices

street, in the **cafés**, at **la gare** and in the

lobby of **votre hôtel**.

So, let's learn how to operate **le téléphone**.

The instructions can look complicated,

but remember, **vous** should be able to

recognize some of these **mots** already. Most

téléphones use **une télécarte. Vous pouvez**
(tay-lay-kart)
telephone card

buy **ces télécartes** at news-stands and in
(say)
these

stores as well as **aux bureaux de poste et**

à la gare. Ready? Well, before you turn
train station

the page it would be a good idea to go back

et review all your numbers one more time.

To dial from the United States to most other countries **vous** need that country's international

area code. Your **annuaire** at home should have a listing of international area codes.
(ah-new-air)
telephone book

Voilà some very useful words built around the word **"téléphone."**

☐	**l'opérateur** *(oh-peh-rah-tur)*	operator	_____
☐	**la cabine téléphonique** *(kah-been)(tay-lay-foh-neek)*	telephone booth	_____
☐	**l'annuaire** *(lah-new-air)*	telephone book	_____
☐	**la conversation téléphonique** *(koh⁽ⁿ⁾-vair-sah-syoh⁽ⁿ⁾)*	telephone conversation	_____

When **vous** leave your contact numbers with friends, family **et** business colleagues, **vous** should include your destination's country code **et** city code whenever possible . For example,

Country Codes		City Codes	
France	33	Paris	1
		Marseille	91
Belgium	32	Brussels	2
		Antwerp	3
Switzerland	41	Geneva	22

To call from one city to another **en France, vous** may need to go to **le bureau de poste ou** call **l'opérateur dans votre hôtel.** Tell **l'opérateur** , "**Je voudrais téléphoner à Chicago,**"
operator

ou "**Je voudrais téléphoner à San Francisco.**"

Now you try it: _____
(I would like to call . . .)

When answering **le téléphone, vous** pick up the receiver **et** say,

> (ah-loh)   (lah-pah-ray)
> "**Allô** c'est _____ **à l'appareil.**"
>   (votre nom)   on the phone

When saying goodbye, **vous dites,** "**Au revoir,**" (ruh-vwahr) **ou** "**À demain.**" (duh-ma(n)) Your turn —
until tomorrow

_____
(Hello. This is . . .)

_____   _____
        (goodbye)   (until tomorrow)

(noo-blee-ay)
N'oubliez pas that **vous pouvez** ask . . .
don't forget   can

(kohm-bya(n)) (koot) (ah-pel)   (oh) (zay-tah-zoo-nee)
Combien coûte un appel téléphonique aux États-Unis? _____
                                         U.S.A.

Combien coûte un appel téléphonique au Canada? _____

Voilà some emergency telephone numbers.

❏	**en France:**	**police** (poh-lees)	police	17	_____
		feu (fuh)	fire	18	_____
❏	**en Suisse:**	**police** (poh-lees)	police	117	_____
		feu (fuh)	fire	118	_____

Voilà some sample sentences for **le téléphone.** Write them in the blanks **en bas.**

(voo-dray) *(tay-lay-foh-nay)* *(boh-stoh⁽ⁿ⁾)*
Je voudrais téléphoner à Boston. _____

(lah-ay-roh-por)
Je voudrais téléphoner à Air France à l'aéroport. _____

(oh) *(may-duh-sa⁽ⁿ⁾)*
Je voudrais téléphoner au médecin. _____

(moh⁽ⁿ⁾)
Mon numéro est le (1) 53-68-70-10. _____
my

(kel) *(ay)*
Quel est votre numéro de téléphone? _____
what

Quel est le numéro de téléphone de l'hôtel? _____

Christine: **Allô, c'est Madame Villon à l'appareil.** *(lah-pah-ray)* **Je voudrais parler à Madame**

Beauchamp.

_____

Téléphoniste: **Un instant, s'il vous plaît. Excusez-moi, mais la ligne est occupée.**
one   *(a⁽ⁿ⁾-stah⁽ⁿ⁾)*   *(may)* *(leen-yuh)*
                                                         but   line   busy

_____

Christine: **Répétez, s'il vous plaît. Parlez plus lentement.**
           (ray-pay-tay)   speak   *(plew)* *(lah⁽ⁿ⁾-tuh-mah⁽ⁿ⁾)*
                                                 more   slowly

_____

Téléphoniste: **Excusez-moi, mais la ligne est occupée.**

_____

Christine: **Oh. Merci. Au revoir.**
                     (oh) *(ruh-vwahr)*

_____

Vous êtes ready to use any **téléphone en France.** Just take it **lentement** et speak clearly.
                                                              (lah⁽ⁿ⁾-tuh-mah⁽ⁿ⁾)
                                                              slowly

Voilà countries **vous** may wish to call.
- ☐ **l'Algérie** *(lahl-zhay-ree)* . . . . Algeria   _____
- ☐ **l'Autriche** *(loh-treesh)* . . . . Austria   _____
- ☐ **la Belgique** *(bel-zheek)* . . . . Belgium   _____
- ☐ **le Canada** *(kah-nah-dah)* . . . . Canada   _____

95

An excellent means of transportation **est le métro.** *(may-troh)* **Le métro à Paris est** the quickest **et**

cheapest form of **transport.** *(trah⁽ⁿ⁾-spor)* transportation **Le métro est** an extensive **système** *(see-stem)* which has been expanded by

an express line to the suburbs, **le RER.** *(air-uh-air)* **Il y a toujours l'autobus** *(too-zhoor)* which is a slower but more
there is   always

scenic form of **transport.** *(trah⁽ⁿ⁾-spor)*

le métro *(may-troh)*
subway

l'autobus *(loh-toh-boos)*
bus

la station de métro *(stah-syoh⁽ⁿ⁾)*
station

la station de taxis *(stah-syoh⁽ⁿ⁾) (tahx-ee)*

l'arrêt d'autobus *(lah-ray)*
stop

Maps displaying the various **lignes** *(leen-yuh)* lines **et arrêts** *(ah-ray)* stops **sont généralement** outside every **entrée de** *(ah⁽ⁿ⁾-tray)*

station de métro. Most **plans de Paris** *(plah⁽ⁿ⁾)* map also have a **métro** map. **Les lignes sont** color-
lines

coded to facilitate reading, just like your example on the next page. If **vous devez changer de** *(duh-vay)*
must

train, look for **les correspondances** *(koh-ray-spoh⁽ⁿ⁾-dah⁽ⁿ⁾s)* connections, transfers clearly marked at each station.

☐	**l'Allemagne** *(lahl-mahn-yuh)*	Germany
☐	**l'Angleterre** *(lah⁽ⁿ⁾-gluh-tair)*	England
☐	**l'Espagne** *(leh-spahn-yuh)*	Spain
☐	**l'Irelande** *(leer-lahnd)*	Ireland
☐	**l'Italie** *(lee-tah-lee)*	Italy

Other than having foreign words, **le métro français** functions just like **à Londres ou à New York**. Locate your destination, select the correct line on your practice **métro et** hop on board.

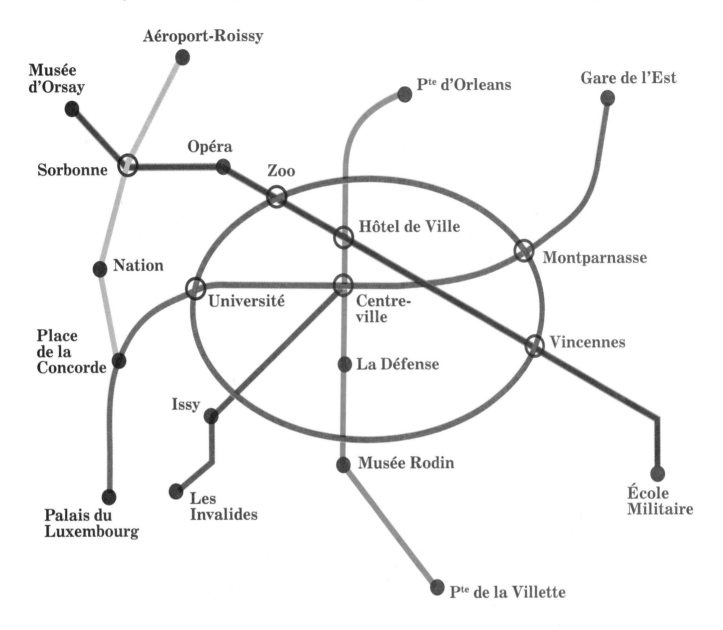

Say these questions aloud many times and don't forget you need **un billet pour le métro!**

> *(stah-syoh⁽ⁿ⁾)* *(may-troh)*
> **Où est la station de métro?**
>
> **Où est la station de taxis?**
>
> **Où est l'arrêt d'autobus?**

❑ **le Luxembourg** *(lewk-sah⁽ⁿ⁾-boor)*	Luxembourg	_____
❑ **les Pays-Bas** *(lay)(pay-ee-bah)*	Netherlands	_____
❑ **l'Afrique du Sud** *(lah-freek)(dew)(sood)*	South Africa	_____
❑ **la Suisse** *(swees)*	Switzerland	_____
❑ **les États-Unis** *(lay)(zay-tah-zoo-nee)*	the United States	_____

Practice the following basic questions out loud **et** then write them in the blanks below.

1. *(kel)* *(fray-kah^(n)s)* *(day)*
   Quelle est la fréquence des trains pour le Louvre? _____
   what   is   frequency/how often

   Quelle est la fréquence des autobus pour Montparnasse? _____

   (lah-ay-roh-por)
   Quelle est la fréquence des trains pour l'aéroport? _____

2. *(kah^(n))* *(par-teel)*
   Quand le train part-il? _____
   when   does it leave

   Quand l'autobus part-il? _____ *Quand l'autobus part-il?* _____

3. *(koot)* *(tee-kay)*
   Combien coûte un ticket de métro? _____

   Combien coûte un ticket d'autobus? _____

   (tah-reef) *(say)*
   Le tarif, c'est combien? _____
   fare   it is   how much

   Le ticket, c'est combien? _____

4. *(oo)* *(stah-syoh^(n))*
   Où est la station de métro? _____

   Où est la station de taxis? _____

   (lah-ray)
   Où est l'arrêt d'autobus? _____

Let's change directions **et** learn **trois** new verbs. **Vous** know the basic "plug-in" formula, so write out your own sentences using these new verbs.

(lah-vay)
laver _____
to wash (clothes)

(pair-druh)
perdre _____
to lose

(eel) (foh)
il faut _____
it is necessary (it takes)

Voilà a few more holidays to keep in mind.
- ☐ **Fête du Travail** *(fet)(dew)(trah-vy)* . . . . Labor Day
- ☐ **Fête Nationale** *(fet)(nah-syoh-nahl)* . . . . National/Bastille Day
- ☐ **Armistice** *(ar-mees-tees)* . . . . Victory Day 1945
- ☐ **Toussaint** *(too-sa^(n)t)* . . . . All Saints' Day (Nov. 1)

23

La Vente et l'Achat
(vah⁽ⁿ⁾t) selling   *(lah-shah)* buying

Shopping abroad is exciting. The simple everyday task of buying **un litre** *(lee-truh)* liter **de lait** *(lay)* milk **ou une**

pomme *(pohm)* apple becomes a challenge that **vous** should **maintenant** be able to meet quickly **et** easily. Of

course, **vous** will purchase **des souvenirs** *(soo-vuh-neer)* souvenirs**, des timbres et des cartes postales** but do not forget

those many other items ranging from shoelaces to **aspirine** *(ah-spee-reen)* aspirin that **vous** might need unexpectedly.

Locate your store, draw a line to it **et**, as always, write your new words in the blanks provided.

le grand magasin *(grah⁽ⁿ⁾)* *(mah-gah-za⁽ⁿ⁾)* department store _____

le cinéma *(see-nay-mah)* cinema _____

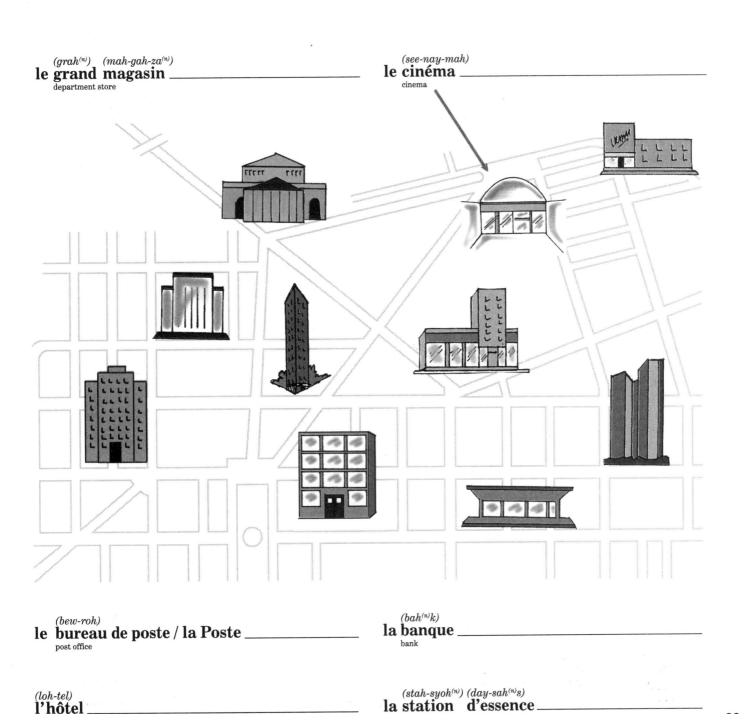

le bureau de poste / la Poste *(bew-roh)* post office _____

la banque *(bah⁽ⁿ⁾k)* bank _____

l'hôtel *(loh-tel)* hotel _____

la station d'essence *(stah-syoh⁽ⁿ⁾)* *(day-sah⁽ⁿ⁾s)* service station _____

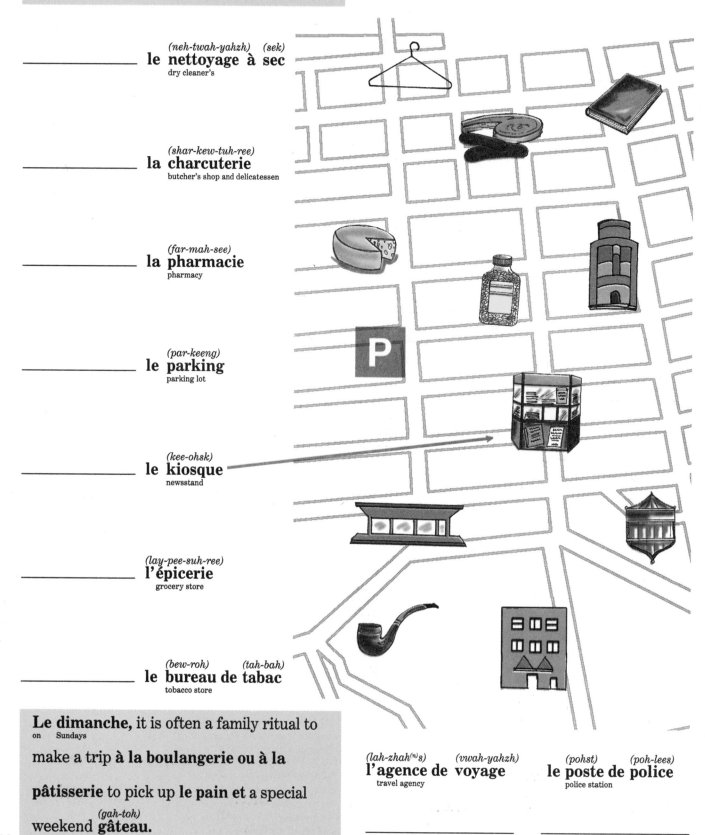

(boo-shuh-ree)
la boucherie
butcher shop

(lee-brair-ree)
la librairie
bookstore

_____   _____

(mah-gah-za⁽ⁿ⁾) *(oo-vair)*
Les magasins sont généralement ouverts de 9:00 à 18:30. Keep in mind that many shops close over the lunch hour.

_____
(neh-twah-yahzh) (sek)
le nettoyage à sec
dry cleaner's

_____
(shar-kew-tuh-ree)
la charcuterie
butcher's shop and delicatessen

_____
(far-mah-see)
la pharmacie
pharmacy

_____
(par-keeng)
le parking
parking lot

_____
(kee-ohsk)
le kiosque
newsstand

_____
(lay-pee-suh-ree)
l'épicerie
grocery store

_____
(bew-roh) (tah-bah)
le bureau de tabac
tobacco store

Le dimanche, it is often a family ritual to
on Sundays
make a trip **à la boulangerie ou à la pâtisserie** to pick up **le pain et** a special weekend *(gah-toh)* **gâteau.**
cake

(lah-zhah⁽ⁿ⁾s) (vwah-yahzh)
l'agence de voyage
travel agency

(pohst) (poh-lees)
le poste de police
police station

_____   _____

100

(lay-tuh-ree)
la laiterie
dairy

_____

(fluhr-eest)
le fleuriste
florist

_____

(pwah-soh(n)-nuh-ree)
la poissonnerie _____
fish shop

(fwee-tee-ay)
le fruitier _____
fruit vendor

(mar-shay)
le marché _____
market

(soo-pair-mar-shay)
le supermarché _____
supermarket

(lor-loh-zhuh-ree)
l'horlogerie _____
watchmaker's shop

(boo-lah(n)-zhuh-ree)
la boulangerie *la boulangerie*
bakery

(pah-tee-suh-ree)
la pâtisserie _____
pastry shop

(lah-vuh-ree) (oh-toh-mah-teek)
la laverie automatique _____
laundromat

(pah-peh-tuh-ree)
la papeterie
stationery store

_____

(kwah-fur)
le coiffeur
hairdresser

_____

En France, the ground floor **s'appelle** "**le**
(ray-duh-shoh-say)   *(pruh-mee-air) (ay-tahzh)*
rez-de-chaussée." The **premier étage**

est the next floor up **et** so on.

24

Le Grand Magasin
(grah⁽ⁿ⁾) *(mah-gah-za⁽ⁿ⁾)*
department store

At this point, **vous** should just about be ready for **votre voyage**. **Vous** have gone shopping for those last-minute odds 'n ends. Most likely, the store directory at your local **grand magasin** did not look like the one **en bas**! **Vous savez** that *(ah⁽ⁿ⁾-fah⁽ⁿ⁾)* **"enfant"** is French for "<u>child</u>" so if **vous avez** *(voo)* *(zah-vay)* **besoin de** something for a child, **vous** would probably look on the **deuxième ou troisième** *(duh-zee-em)* *(twah-zee-em)* second **étage, n'est-ce pas**? *(ay-tahzh)* *(ness)* *(pah)*

4ME ■ ÉTAGE	vaisselle cristal lampes tapis	service de table ameublement de cuisine lits	clés faïence porcelaine miroirs
3ME ■ ÉTAGE	disques télévisions meubles d'enfant jouets	radios instruments de musique papeterie	tabac restaurant journaux revues
2ME ■ ÉTAGE	tout pour l'enfant vêtements de femme chapeaux de femme	vêtements d'homme chaussures d'enfant photos livres	toilettes antiquités ameublement tableaux

1ER ■ ÉTAGE	accessoires d'auto
	lingerie
	mouchoirs
	maillots de bain
		chaussures de
		  femme
		chaussures d'homme
			équipement de
			  sport
			outils
			mobilier de camping

R	parapluies cartes chapeaux d'homme bijouterie	gants maroquinerie chaussettes ceintures	pendules/montres parfumerie confiserie caféteria

Let's start a checklist **pour votre voyage**. Besides **vêtements, de quoi avez-vous besoin?** As *(vet-mah⁽ⁿ⁾)* *(kwah)* your clothing what you learn these **mots,** assemble these items **dans un coin** of your **maison.** Check **et** make sure *(kwa⁽ⁿ⁾)* corner that they **sont propres et** ready **pour votre voyage.** Be sure to do the same **avec le reste des** *(proh-pruh)* *(rehst)* clean with rest of the **choses** that **vous** pack. On the next pages, match each item to its picture, draw a line to it and things write out the word many times. As **vous** organize these things, check them off on this list. Do not forget to take the next group of sticky labels and label these **choses aujourd'hui.** today

(pahs-por)
le passeport
passport

(bee-yay)
le billet
ticket

(vah-leez)
la valise
suitcase

la valise, la valise, la valise ✔

(sahk)(ah)(ma⁽ⁿ⁾)
le sac à main
handbag

(port-fuh-yuh)
le portefeuille
wallet

(lar-zhah⁽ⁿ⁾)
l'argent
money

(kart) *(kray-dee)*
les cartes de crédit
credit cards

(shek) *(vwah-yahzh)*
les chèques de voyage
traveler's checks

(lah-pah-ray-foh-toh)
l'appareil-photo
camera

(peh-lee-kewl)
la pellicule
film

(my-oh) *(ba⁽ⁿ⁾)*
le maillot de bain
swim trunks

(my-oh) *(ba⁽ⁿ⁾)*
le maillot de bain
swimsuit

(sah⁽ⁿ⁾-dahl)
les sandales
sandals

(lew-net) *(soh-lay)*
les lunettes de soleil
sunglasses

(brohs) *(dah⁽ⁿ⁾)*
la brosse à dents
toothbrush

(dah⁽ⁿ⁾-tee-frees)
le dentifrice
toothpaste

(sah-voh⁽ⁿ⁾)
le savon
soap

(rah-zwahr)
le rasoir
razor

(day-oh-doh-rah⁽ⁿ⁾)
le déodorant
deodorant

le peigne *(pen-yuh)*
comb

le manteau *(mah(n)-toh)*
raincoat

le parapluie *(pah-rah-plew-ee)*
umbrella

l'imperméable *(la(n)-pair-may-ah-bluh)*
overcoat

les gants *(gah(n))*
gloves

le chapeau *(shah-poh)*
hat

le chapeau *(shah-poh)*
hat

les bottes *(boht)*
boots

les chaussures *(shoh-suhr)*
shoes

les tennis *(teh-nees)*
tennis shoes

le complet *(koh(n)-play)*
suit

la cravate *(krah-vaht)*
tie

la chemise *(shuh-meez)*
shirt

le mouchoir *(moo-shwahr)*
handkerchief

le veston *(veh-stoh(n))*
jacket, blazer

le pantalon *(pah(n)-tah-loh(n))*
trousers

le jean *(jean)*
jeans

le short *(short)*
shorts

le teeshirt *(tee-shirt)*
T-shirt

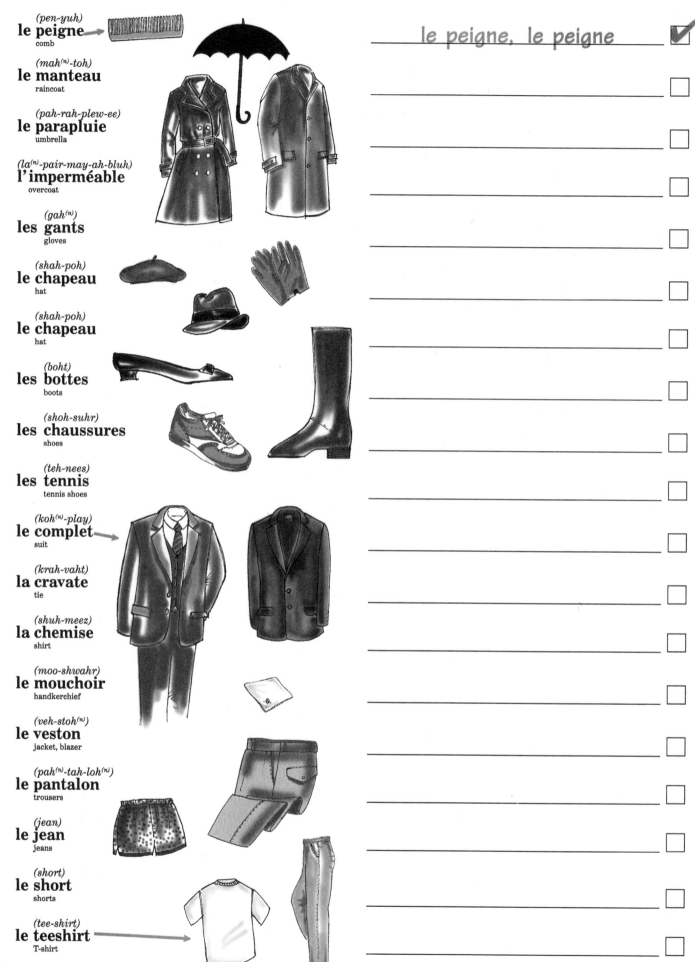

le peigne, le peigne ✓

le slip *(sleep)*
underpants

☐

le maillot de corps *(my-oh) (kor)*
undershirt

☐

le chemisier *(shuh-me-zee-air)*
blouse

☐

la robe *(rohb)*
dress

☐

la jupe *(zhewp)*
skirt

la jupe, la jupe, la jupe   ✔

le pull *(pul)*
sweater

☐

la combinaison *(koh(n)-bee-nay-zoh(n))*
slip

☐

le soutien-gorge *(soo-tya(n)-gorzh)*
brassiere

☐

le slip *(sleep)*
underpants

☐

les chaussettes *(shoh-set)*
socks

☐

les bas *(bah)*
pantyhose

☐

le pyjama *(pee-zhah-mah)*
pajamas

☐

la chemise de nuit *(shuh-meez) (nwee)*
nightshirt

☐

la robe de chambre *(rohb) (shah(n)-bruh)*
bathrobe

☐

les pantoufles *(pah(n)-too-fluh)*
slippers

☐

From now on, **vous avez** *(sah-voh(n))* **"savon" et non pas** "soap." Having assembled these **choses,** *(shohz)* **vous**
you   have   things

are ready **voyager.** Let's add these important shopping phrases to your basic repertoire.
to travel

Quelle taille? *(kel) (tie)* _____
what   size

Ça me va bien. *(sah) (muh) (vah)* _____
it fits me well

Ça ne me va pas. *(nuh) (muh) (vah) (pah)* _____
it does not fit me

Treat yourself to a final review. **Vous savez** *(sah-vay)* **les noms pour les magasins français**, so let's

know

practice shopping. Just remember your key question **mots** that you learned in Step 2. Whether

vous need to buy **un chapeau** *(shah-poh)* **ou un livre** the necessary **mots** are the same.

1. First step — **où?**

Où est la laiterie? *(lay-tuh-ree)*   **Où est la banque?** *(bah$^{(n)}$k)*   **Où est le kiosque?** *(kee-ohsk)*

_____

(Where is the department store?)

_____

(Where is the grocery store?)

_____

(Where is the market?)

2. Second step — tell them what **vous** are looking for, need **ou voulez!** *(voo-lay)*

want

J'ai besoin de . . .   **Je voudrais . . .**   **Avez-vous . . . ?**

I need   *I   would like*   *do you have*

_____

(Do you have postcards?)

_____

(I want four stamps.)

_____

(I need toothpaste.)

_____

(I want to buy film.)

_____

(Do you have coffee?)

Go through the glossary at the end of this **livre et** select **vingt mots.** Drill the above patterns

avec *(say)* **ces vingt mots.** Don't cheat. Drill them **aujourd'hui. Maintenant,** take *(ah⁽ⁿ⁾-kor)* **encore vingt**
these   more

mots de votre glossary **et** do the same.

3. Third step — find out **combien** *(kohm-bya⁽ⁿ⁾)* **ça** *(sah)* **coûte.** *(koot)*

Combien *(ess)* **est-ce?**   **Combien** *(sah)* **ça** *(koot)* **coûte?**   **Combien** *(koot)* **coûte le** *(kray-yoh⁽ⁿ⁾)* **crayon?**

_____ (How much does the toothpaste cost?) _____

_____ (How much does the soap cost?) _____

_____ (How much does a cup of tea cost?) _____

4.   Fourth step — success! I found it!

Once **vous trouvez** what **vous** would like, **vous** *(deet)* **dites,**
say

Je voudrais ça, s'il vous plaît. _____

or

Je le *(prah⁽ⁿ⁾)* **prends,** *(seel)* **s'il vous plaît.** _____
take

Ou if **vous** would not like it, **vous dites,**

Je ne *(vuh)* **veux pas ça, merci.** _____
want

or

Je ne le prends pas, merci. _____
do not take

Congratulations! You have finished. By now you should have stuck your labels, flashed your

cards, cut out your menu guide and packed your suitcases. You should be very pleased with your

accomplishment. You have learned what it sometimes takes others years to achieve and you

hopefully had fun doing it. *(boh⁽ⁿ⁾)* **Bon voyage!**

Glossary

This glossary contains words used in this book only. It is not meant to be a dictionary. Consider purchasing a dictionary which best suits your needs - small for traveling, large for reference, or specialized for specific vocabulary needs.

Remember that French adjectives can have different endings depending upon whether they are used in their feminine or masculine form. The masculine form is given here. The (e) following the masculine form indicates that this word's feminine form simply adds an "e." If the feminine form is significantly different, it will be given in its entirety. Learn to look for the core of the word.

A

à *(ah)* .... at, to, in
  à côté de *(ah)(koh-tay)(duh)* .... next to
  à la française *(ah)(lah)(frah$^{(n)}$-sez)* .. in the French manner
accepter *(ahk-sep-tay)* .... to accept
accident, le *(ahk-see-dah$^{(n)}$)* .... accident
achat, le *(ah-shah)* .... purchase
acheter *(ah-shuh-tay)* .... to buy
addition, la *(ah-dee-syoh$^{(n)}$)* ...... bill in a restaurant
admission, la *(ahd-mee-syoh$^{(n)}$)* .... admission
adresse, la *(ah-dress)* .... address
aéroport, le *(ah-ay-roh-por)* .... airport
Afrique, la *(ah-freek)* .... Africa
Afrique du Sud, la *(ah-freek)(dew)(sood)* ..... South Africa
agence de location des voitures, la *(ah-zhah$^{(n)}$s)(duh)(loh-kah-syoh$^{(n)}$)(duh)(vwah-tewr)* .... car-rental agency
agence de voyage, la *(ah-zhah$^{(n)}$s)(duh)(vwah-yahzh)* .... travel agency
agneau, le *(ahn-yoh)* .... lamb
aidez-moi *(ay-day-mwah)* .... help me! aid me!
alcool, le *(ahl-kohl)* .... alcohol
Algérie, la *(ahl-zhay-ree)* .... Algeria
Allemagne, la *(ahl-mahn-yuh)* .... Germany
allemand (e) *(ahl-mah$^{(n)}$)* .... German
aller *(ah-lay)* .... to go
aller-retour, le *(ah-lay-ruh-tour)* ..... round-trip ticket
aller simple, le *(ah-lay)(sa$^{(n)}$-pluh)* .... one-way ticket
allô *(ah-loh)* .... hello (on telephone)
Alpes, les *(ahlp)* .... the Alps
alphabet, le *(ahl-fah-bay)* .... alphabet
américain (e) *(ah-may-ree-ka$^{(n)}$)* .... American
Amérique, la *(ah-may-reek)* .... America
amusez-vous *(ah-mew-zay-voo)* .... enjoy yourself!
an, le *(ah$^{(n)}$)* .... year
ancien (ancienne) *(ah$^{(n)}$-syah$^{(n)}$)* .... old
anglais (e) *(ah$^{(n)}$-glay)* .... English
Angleterre, la *(ah$^{(n)}$-gluh-tair)* .... England
animal, le *(ah-nee-mahl)* .... animal
année, la *(ah-nay)* .... year
annuaire, le *(ah-new-air)* .... telephone book
août, le *(oot)* .... August
appareil, le *(ah-pah-ray)* .... gadget, appliance
appareil-photo, le *(ah-pah-ray-foh-toh)* .... camera
appartement, le *(ah-par-teh-mah$^{(n)}$)* .... apartment
appel, le *(ah-pel)* .... call
appel téléphonique, le *(ah-pel)(tay-lay-foh-neek)* .. telephone call
s'appeler *(sah-puh-lay)* .... to be called
  Comment vous appelez-vous? *(koh-moh$^{(n)}$)(voo)(zah-puh-lay-voo)* .... What is your name?
  je m'appelle *(zhuh)(mah-pel)* .... my name is
appétit, le *(ah-pay-tee)* .... appetite
apprendre *(ah-prah$^{(n)}$-druh)* .... to learn
après-midi, le *(ah-preh-mee-dee)* .... afternoon
argent, le *(ar-zhah$^{(n)}$)* .... money

armoire, la *(ar-mwahr)* .... closet, wardrobe
arrêt, le *(ah-ray)* .... stop, arrest
arrivée, la *(ah-ree-vay)* .... arrival
arriver *(ah-ree-vay)* .... to arrive
aspirine, la *(ah-spee-reen)* .... aspirin
assiette, la *(ah-syet)* .... plate
assis (e) *(ah-see)* .... seated
attendre *(ah-tah$^{(n)}$-druh)* .... to wait for
attention, la *(ah-tah$^{(n)}$-syoh$^{(n)}$)* .... attention
au *(oh)* .... in, in the, at the
  au-dessus de *(oh-duh-syoo)(duh)* .... over
  au revoir *(oh)(ruh-vwahr)* .... goodbye
auberge, la *(oh-bairzh)* .... country inn
aujourd'hui *(oh-zhoor-dwee)* .... today
aussi *(oh-see)* .... also
auteur, le *(oh-tur)* .... author
auto, la *(oh-toh)* .... car
autobus, le *(oh-toh-boos)* .... bus
automne, le *(oh-tohn)* .... autumn
autorail, le *(oh-toh-rye)* .... slow train
autoroute, la *(oh-toh-root)* .... freeway
Autriche, la *(oh-treesh)* .... Austria
avec *(ah-vek)* .... with
avez *(ah-vay)* .... (you) have
avion, le *(ah-vyoh$^{(n)}$)* .... airplane
avoir *(ah-vwahr)* .... to have
  j'ai *(zhay)* .... I have
  nous avons *(noo)(zah-voh$^{(n)}$)* .... we have
avoir besoin de *(ah-vwahr)(buh-zwa$^{(n)}$)(duh)* ...... to need
avril *(ah-vreel)* .... April

B

balcon, le *(bahl-koh$^{(n)}$)* .... balcony
ballet, le *(bah-leh)* .... ballet
ballon, le *(bah-loh$^{(n)}$)* .... balloon, big ball
banane, la *(bah-nahn)* .... banana
banc, le *(bah$^{(n)}$)* .... bench
banque, la *(bah$^{(n)}$k)* .... bank
bar, le *(bar)* .... type of café/restaurant
bas *(bah)* .... low
  en bas *(ah$^{(n)}$)(bah)* .... below, downstairs
bas, les *(bah)* .... pantyhose
bateau, le *(bah-toh)* .... boat
beau *(boh)* .... beautiful
beaucoup *(boh-koo)* .... many, a lot
Belgique, la *(bel-zheek)* .... Belgium
belle *(bel)* .... beautiful
besoin, le *(buh-zwa$^{(n)}$)* .... need
beurre, le *(buhr)* .... butter
bicyclette, la *(bee-see-klet)* .... bicycle
bien *(bya$^{(n)}$)* .... well
  pas bien *(pah)(bya$^{(n)}$)* .... not too well
bien sûr *(bya$^{(n)}$)(sur)* .... of course
bière, la *(bee-air)* .... beer
bifteck, le *(beef-tek)* .... beefsteak

108

billet, le *(bee-ay)* . . . . bank note, ticket
biscuit, le *(bee-skwee)* . . . . cookie
bistro, le *(bee-stroh)* . . . . café, restaurant
blanc (blanche) *(blah⁽ⁿ⁾)* . . . . white
bleu (e) *(bluh)* . . . . blue
boeuf, le *(buf)* . . . . beef
boire *(bwahr)* . . . . to drink
boisson, la *(bwah-soh⁽ⁿ⁾)* . . . . beverage
boîte aux lettres, la *(bwaht)(oh)(let-ruh)* . . . . mailbox
bon *(boh⁽ⁿ⁾)* . . . . good
 bon appétit *(boh⁽ⁿ⁾)(nah-pay-tee)* . . . . . . enjoy your meal
 bon marché *(boh⁽ⁿ⁾)(mar-shay)* . . . . inexpensive
bonjour *(boh⁽ⁿ⁾)(zhoor)* . . . . good morning, good day
bonne *(bun)* . . . . good
 bonne chance *(bun)(shah⁽ⁿ⁾s)* . . . . good luck
 bonne nuit *(bun)(nwee)* . . . . good night
bonsoir *(boh⁽ⁿ⁾-swahr)* . . . . good evening
botte, la *(boht)* . . . . boot
boucherie, la *(boo-shuh-ree)* . . . . butcher shop
boulangerie, la *(boo-lah⁽ⁿ⁾-zhuh-ree)* . . . . bakery
bouteille, la *(boo-tay)* . . . . bottle
brasserie, la *(brah-suh-ree)* . . . . restaurant
bref (brève) *(brehf)* . . . . brief, short
brillant (e) *(bree-yah⁽ⁿ⁾)* . . . . brilliant, sparkling
brosse à dents, la *(brohs)(ah)(dah⁽ⁿ⁾)* . . . . . . toothbrush
brouillard, le *(broo-ee-yar)* . . . . fog
bureau, le *(bew-roh)* . . . . desk, office
bureau de change, le *(bew-roh)(duh)(shah⁽ⁿ⁾zh)* . . . .
. . . . money-exchange counter
bureau de poste, le *(bew-roh)(duh)(pohst)* . . . . . . post office
bureau de tabac, le *(bew-roh)(duh)(tah-bah)* . . . tobacco store
bureau des objets trouvés, le *(bew-roh)(day)(zohb-zhay)*
(troo-vay) . . . . lost-and-found office

C

c'est *(say)* . . . . it is
c'était *(say-tay)* . . . . it was
ça *(sah)* . . . . that, it
ça me va bien *(sah)(muh)(vah)(bya⁽ⁿ⁾)* . . . . it fits me
cabine téléphonique, la *(kah-been)(tay-lay-foh-neek)* . . . . .
. . . . telephone booth
café, le *(kah-fay)* . . . . coffee, café
caisse, la *(kess)* . . . . cashier, register
calendrier, le *(kah-lah⁽ⁿ⁾-dree-ay)* . . . . calendar
Canada, le *(kah-nah-dah)* . . . . Canada
canadien (canadienne) *(kah-nah-dya⁽ⁿ⁾)* . . . . Canadian
canapé, le *(kah-nah-pay)* . . . . sofa
capitale, la *(kah-pee-tahl)* . . . . capital
carafe, la *(kah-rahf)* . . . . carafe
carte, la *(kart)* . . . . menu, map
carte de crédit, la *(kart)(duh)(kray-dee)* . . . . . . credit card
carte postale, la *(kart)(poh-stahl)* . . . . postcard
casse-croûte, le *(kahs-kroot)* . . . . snack
cathédrale, la *(kah-tay-drahl)* . . . . cathedral
catholique *(kah-toh-leek)* . . . . Catholic
ce, cette *(suh), (set)* . . . . that, this
Celsius *(sel-see-ews)* . . . . Centigrade
cendrier, le *(sah⁽ⁿ⁾-dree-ay)* . . . . ashtray
cent *(sah⁽ⁿ⁾)* . . . . one hundred
centime, le *(sah⁽ⁿ⁾-teem)* . . . . centime (part of a franc)
centre, le *(sah⁽ⁿ⁾-truh)* . . . . center
ces *(say)* . . . . these, those
chaise, la *(shehz)* . . . . chair
chambre, la *(shah⁽ⁿ⁾-bruh)* . . . . room
chambre à coucher, la *(shah⁽ⁿ⁾-bruh)(ah)(koo-shay)* . . . .
. . . . bedroom
champagne, le *(shah⁽ⁿ⁾-pahn-yuh)* . . . . champagne

changement, le *(shah⁽ⁿ⁾-zhuh-mah⁽ⁿ⁾)* . . . . change
changer (de train, d'autobus) *(shah⁽ⁿ⁾-zhay)* . . . .
. . . . to transfer, change (train, bus)
chapeau, le *(shah-poh)* . . . . hat
charcuterie, la *(shar-kew-tuh-ree)* . . . butcher's shop and deli
chat, le *(shah)* . . . . cat
château, le *(shah-toh)* . . . . castle
chaud (e) *(shoh)* . . . . hot
chaussette, la *(shoh-set)* . . . . sock
chaussure, la *(shoh-suhr)* . . . . shoe
chemise, la *(shuh-meez)* . . . . shirt
chemisier, le *(shuh-me-zee-air)* . . . . blouse
chemise de nuit, la *(shuh-meez)(duh)(nwee)* . . . . nightshirt
chèque, le *(shek)* . . . . bank check
chèque de voyage, le *(shek)(duh)(vwah-yahzh)* . . . .
. . . . traveler's check
cher (chère) *(shair)* . . . . expensive
chercher *(shair-shay)* . . . . to look for
chien, le *(shya⁽ⁿ⁾)* . . . . dog
Chine, la *(sheen)* . . . . China
chocolat, le *(shoh-koh-lah)* . . . . chocolate
chose, la *(shohz)* . . . . thing
cinéma, le *(see-nay-mah)* . . . . cinema
cinq *(sank)* . . . . five
cinquante *(sang-kah⁽ⁿ⁾t)* . . . . fifty
coiffeur, le *(kwah-fur)* . . . . hairdresser
coin, le *(kwa⁽ⁿ⁾)* . . . . corner
combien *(kohm-bya⁽ⁿ⁾)* . . . . how much
 Combien est-ce? *(kohm-bya⁽ⁿ⁾)(ess)* . . . . . . How much is it?
combinaison, la *(koh⁽ⁿ⁾-bee-nay-zoh⁽ⁿ⁾)* . . . slip (undergarment)
commander *(koh-mah⁽ⁿ⁾-day)* . . . . to order
comme *(kohm)* . . . . as
commencer *(koh-mah⁽ⁿ⁾-say)* . . . . to begin, commence
comment *(koh-mah⁽ⁿ⁾)* . . . . how
 Comment allez-vous? *(koh-moh⁽ⁿ⁾)(tah-lay-voo)* . . . .
. . . . How are you?
compagnie, la *(koh⁽ⁿ⁾-pahn-yee)* . . . . company
compartiment, le *(koh⁽ⁿ⁾-par-tuh-mah⁽ⁿ⁾)* . . . . . compartment
complet, le *(koh⁽ⁿ⁾-play)* . . . . suit (clothes)
comprendre *(koh⁽ⁿ⁾-prah⁽ⁿ⁾-druh)* . . . . to understand
compris (e) *(koh⁽ⁿ⁾-pree)* . . . . included
concert, le *(koh⁽ⁿ⁾-sair)* . . . . concert
concierge, le/la *(koh⁽ⁿ⁾-see-airzh)* . . . doorkeeper, concierge
confiture, la *(koh⁽ⁿ⁾-fee-tewr)* . . . . jam
consigne, la *(koh⁽ⁿ⁾-seen-yuh)* . . . . left-luggage office
continuer *(koh⁽ⁿ⁾-tee-new-ay)* . . . . to continue
contravention, la *(koh⁽ⁿ⁾-trah-vah⁽ⁿ⁾-syoh⁽ⁿ⁾)* . . parking ticket
conversation, la *(koh⁽ⁿ⁾-vair-sah-syoh⁽ⁿ⁾)* . . . . conversation
corbeille à papier, la *(kor-bay)(ah)(pah-pee-ay)* . . wastebasket
correspondances, les *(koh-ray-spoh⁽ⁿ⁾-dah⁽ⁿ⁾s)* . . connections
côté, la *(koht)* . . . . coast
couchette, la *(koo-shet)* . . . . berth, bunk
couleur, la *(koo-luhr)* . . . . color
courrier, le *(koo-ree-ay)* . . . . mail
court (e) *(koor)* . . . . short
cousin, le *(koo-za⁽ⁿ⁾)* . . . . cousin (male)
cousine, la *(koo-zeen)* . . . . cousin (female)
couteau, le *(koo-toh)* . . . . knife
coûter *(koo-tay)* . . . . to cost
coutume, la *(koo-tewm)* . . . . custom, habit
couverture, la *(koo-vair-tewr)* . . . . blanket
cravate, la *(krah-vaht)* . . . . necktie
crayon, le *(kray-yoh⁽ⁿ⁾)* . . . . pencil
croissant, le *(kwah-sah⁽ⁿ⁾)* . . . . crescent roll
cuillère, la *(kwee-air)* . . . . spoon
cuisine, la *(kwee-zeen)* . . . . kitchen
cuisinière, la *(kwee-zeen-yair)* . . . . stove

cuit (e) *(kwee)* . . . . cooked
cuit au four *(kwee)(toh)(foor)* . . . . baked

D

dame, la *(dahm)* . . . . lady
dans *(dah⁽ⁿ⁾)* . . . . in, into
danse, la *(dah⁽ⁿ⁾s)* . . . . dance
d', de *(duh)* . . . . of, from, out of, some
de l', de la *(duh)(lah)* . . . . of, from, out of, some
de rien *(duh)(rya⁽ⁿ⁾)* . . . . you're welcome
décembre, le *(day-sah⁽ⁿ⁾m-bruh)* . . . . December
déclaration, la *(day-klah-rah-syoh⁽ⁿ⁾)* . . . . declaration
degré, le *(duh-gray)* . . . . degree
déjà *(day-zhah)* . . . . already
déjà vu *(day-zhah)(vew)* . . . . already seen
déjeuner, le *(day-zhuh-nay)* . . . . lunch
délicieux (délicieuse) *(day-lee-syuh)* . . . . delicious
demain *(duh-ma⁽ⁿ⁾)* . . . . tomorrow
demander *(duh-mah⁽ⁿ⁾-day)* . . . . to ask, ask for
demi (e) *(duh-mee)* . . . . half
dentifrice, le *(dah⁽ⁿ⁾-tee-frees)* . . . . toothpaste
déodorant, le *(day-oh-doh-rah⁽ⁿ⁾)* . . . . deodorant
départ, le *(day-par)* . . . . departure
derrière *(dair-ee-air)* . . . . behind
des *(day)* . . . . some, from the
désir, le *(day-zeer)* . . . . desire
désoler *(day-zoh-lay)* . . . . to distress
je suis désolé *(zhuh)(swee)(day-zoh-lay)* . . . . . . I'm sorry
dessert, le *(day-sair)* . . . . dessert
deux *(duh)* . . . . two
deuxième *(duh-zee-em)* . . . . second
devant *(duh-vah⁽ⁿ⁾)* . . . . in front of
déviation, la *(day-vee-ah-syoh⁽ⁿ⁾)* . . . . detour
devoir *(duh-vwahr)* . . . . to have to, must
dictionnaire, le *(deek-syoh-nair)* . . . . dictionary
différent (e) *(dee-fay-rah⁽ⁿ⁾)* . . . . different
difficile *(dee-fee-seel)* . . . . difficult
dimanche, le *(dee-mah⁽ⁿ⁾sh)* . . . . Sunday
dîner, le *(dee-nay)* . . . . dinner
dire *(deer)* . . . . to say
direction, la *(dee-rek-syoh⁽ⁿ⁾)* . . . . direction
distance, la *(dee-stah⁽ⁿ⁾s)* . . . . distance
dit *(dee)* . . . . says
on dit *(oh⁽ⁿ⁾)(dee)* . . . . one says
dix *(deess)* . . . . ten
dix-huit *(deez-wheat)* . . . . eighteen
dix-neuf *(deez-nuf)* . . . . nineteen
dix-sept *(deez-set)* . . . . seventeen
docteur, le *(dohk-tur)* . . . . doctor
donc *(doh⁽ⁿ⁾k)* . . . . therefore
donnez-moi *(doh⁽ⁿ⁾-nay-mwah)* . . . . give me!
dormir *(dor-meer)* . . . . to sleep
douane, la *(doo-ah⁽ⁿ⁾)* . . . . customs
douche, la *(doosh)* . . . . shower
douze *(dooz)* . . . . twelve
drapeau, le *(drah-poh)* . . . . flag
droite *(dwaht)* . . . . right
du *(dew)* . . . . some, in the, from the

E

eau, la *(oh)* . . . . water
école, la *(ay-kohl)* . . . . school
économie, la *(ay-koh-noh-mee)* . . . . economy
Écosse, la *(ay-kohs)* . . . . Scotland
écrire *(ay-kreer)* . . . . to write
écrivez-moi *(ay-kree-vay-mwah)* . . . . write for me!
110 église, la *(ay-gleez)* . . . . church

elle *(el)* . . . . it, she
elles *(el)* . . . . they
en *(ah⁽ⁿ⁾)* . . . . in, to, into
en anglais *(ah⁽ⁿ⁾)(ah⁽ⁿ⁾-glay)* . . . . in English
en français *(ah⁽ⁿ⁾)(frah⁽ⁿ⁾-say)* . . . . in French
encore *(ah⁽ⁿ⁾-kor)* . . . . again, still, more
enfant, le *(ah⁽ⁿ⁾-fah⁽ⁿ⁾)* . . . . child
entre *(ah⁽ⁿ⁾-truh)* . . . . between
entrée, la *(ah⁽ⁿ⁾-tray)* . . . . entry
entrée principale, la *(ah⁽ⁿ⁾-tray)(pra⁽ⁿ⁾-see-pahl)* . . main entry
entrer *(ah⁽ⁿ⁾-tray)* . . . . to go in, enter
environ *(ah⁽ⁿ⁾-vee-roh⁽ⁿ⁾)* . . . . about
envoyer *(ah⁽ⁿ⁾-vwah-yay)* . . . . to send
épicerie, la *(ay-pee-suh-ree)* . . . . grocery store
escargot, le *(ess-kar-goh)* . . . . snail
Espagne, la *(eh-spahn-yuh)* . . . . Spain
espagnol (e) *(eh-spahn-yohl)* . . . . Spanish
est *(ay)* . . . . (it) is
est-ce *(ess)* . . . . is it, it is
est, le *(est)* . . . . east
et *(ay)* . . . . and
étage, le *(ay-tahzh)* . . . . floor, story
était *(ay-tay)* . . . . (it) was
état, le *(ay-tah)* . . . . state
États-Unis, les *(ay-tah-zoo-nee)* . . . . USA
été, le *(ay-tay)* . . . . summer
êtes *(et)* . . . . (you) are
étions *(ay-tee-oh⁽ⁿ⁾)* . . . . (we) were
étranger (étrangère) *(ay-trah⁽ⁿ⁾-zhay)* . . . . foreign, abroad
être *(et-ruh)* . . . . to be
Europe, la *(uh-rohp)* . . . . Europe
européen (européenne) *(uh-roh-pay-yen)* . . . . . European
excellent (e) *(ek-suh-lah⁽ⁿ⁾)* . . . . excellent
excusez-moi *(ek-skew-zay-mwah)* . . . . excuse me
exemple, le *(eg-zah⁽ⁿ⁾-pluh)* . . . . example
express, le *(ek-spress)* . . . . fast train
extrêmement *(ek-streh-muh-mah⁽ⁿ⁾)* . . . . extremely

F

facile *(fah-seel)* . . . . easy
facture, la *(fahk-tewr)* . . . . bill in hotel
faim, la *(fa⁽ⁿ⁾)* . . . . hunger
faire *(fair)* . . . . to do, make
fait *(fay)* . . . . (it) makes
faire les valises *(fair)(lay)(vah-leez)* . . . . to pack
famille, la *(fah-mee-yuh)* . . . . family
farci (e) *(far-see)* . . . . stuffed
fatigue, la *(fah-teeg)* . . . . fatigue, tiredness
fax, le *(fahx)* . . . . fax
femme, la *(fahm)* . . . . woman
fenêtre, la *(fuh-net-ruh)* . . . . window
fermé (e) *(fair-may)* . . . . closed
festival, le *(feh-stee-vahl)* . . . . festival
fête, la *(fet)* . . . . feast, festival
feu, le *(fuh)* . . . . fire
février, le *(fah-vree-ay)* . . . . February
fille, la *(fee-yuh)* . . . . girl, daughter
film, le *(feelm)* . . . . film
fils, le *(feess)* . . . . son
filtre, le *(feel-truh)* . . . . filter
fin, la *(fa⁽ⁿ⁾)* . . . . end
fleur, la *(fluhr)* . . . . flower
fleuriste, le *(fluhr-eest)* . . . . florist
foi, la *(fwah)* . . . . faith
fonctionnaire, le *(foh⁽ⁿ⁾-syoh⁽ⁿ⁾-nair)* . . functionary, civil servant
football, le *(foot-bahl)* . . . . soccer
forêt, la *(foh-ray)* . . . . forest

forme, la *(form)* . . . . form, shape
fourchette, la *(foor-shet)* . . . . fork
foyer, le *(fwah-yay)* . . . . home, hearth, lobby
frais (fraîche) *(fray)* . . . . fresh, cool
franc (franche) *(frah⁽ⁿ⁾)* . . . . frank, honest
franc, le *(frah⁽ⁿ⁾)* . . . . franc
français (e) *(frah⁽ⁿ⁾-say)* . . . . French
Français, les *(frah⁽ⁿ⁾-say)* . . . . the French people
France, la *(frah⁽ⁿ⁾s)* . . . . France
fréquence, la *(fray-kah⁽ⁿ⁾s)* . . . . frequency
frère, le *(frair)* . . . . brother
frit (e) *(free)* . . . . fried
froid (e) *(fwah)* . . . . cold
fromage, le *(froh-mahzh)* . . . . cheese
fruit, le *(fwee)* . . . . fruit
fruitier, le *(fwee-tee-ay)* . . . . fruit vendor
fumé *(few-may)* . . . . smoked
fumer *(few-may)* . . . . to smoke

G

galerie, la *(gah-leh-ree)* . . . . gallery, long room
gant, le *(gah⁽ⁿ⁾)* . . . . glove
garage, le *(gah-rahzh)* . . . . garage
garçon, le *(gar-soh⁽ⁿ⁾)* . . . . boy, waiter
gare, la *(gar)* . . . . train station
gâteau, le *(gah-toh)* . . . . cake
gauche *(gohsh)* . . . . left
généralement *(zhah-nay-rahl-mah⁽ⁿ⁾)* . . . . generally
géographie, la *(zhay-oh-grah-fee)* . . . . geography
gibier, le *(zhee-bee-ay)* . . . . wild game
glace, la *(glahs)* . . . . ice, ice cream
gomme, la *(gohm)* . . . . eraser
gourmand, le *(goor-mah⁽ⁿ⁾)* . . . . gourmand, glutton
gourmet, le *(goor-may)* . . . . gourmet
gouvernement, le *(goo-vair-nuh-mah⁽ⁿ⁾)* . . . . . government
grand (e) *(grah⁽ⁿ⁾)* . . . . big, large, tall
grand-mère, la *(grah⁽ⁿ⁾-mair)* . . . . grandmother
grand-père, le *(grah⁽ⁿ⁾-pair)* . . . . grandfather
grands-parents, les *(grah⁽ⁿ⁾-pah-rah⁽ⁿ⁾)* . . . grandparents
grandeur, la *(grah⁽ⁿ⁾-dur)* . . . . greatness
grillé (e) *(gree-ay)* . . . . grilled
gris (e) *(gree)* . . . . gray
guichet, le *(ghee-shay)* . . . . counter, window
guide, le *(geed)* . . . . guide

H

habiter *(ah-bee-tay)* . . . . to live, reside
haut (e) *(oh)* . . . . high
en haut *(ah⁽ⁿ⁾)(oh)* . . . . above, upstairs
heure, la *(uhr)* . . . . hour
hier *(ee-air)* . . . . yesterday
hiver, le *(ee-vair)* . . . . winter
homme, le *(ohm)* . . . . man
horaire, le *(oh-rair)* . . . . timetable
horloge, la *(or-lohzh)* . . . . large clock
horlogerie, la *(or-loh-zhuh-ree)* . . . . watchmaker's shop
hors-d'oeuvre, le *(or-duh-vruh)* . . . . appetizers
hôtel, le *(oh-tel)* . . . . hotel
hôtelier, le *(oh-tel-yay)* . . . . hotelkeeper
huit *(wheat)* . . . . eight

I

ici *(ee-see)* . . . . here
idée, la *(ee-day)* . . . . idea
identification, la *(ee-dah⁽ⁿ⁾-tee-fee-kah-syoh⁽ⁿ⁾)* . . identification
il *(eel)* . . . . it, he
il faut *(eel)(foh)* . . . . it is necessary

il n'y a pas de quoi *(eel)(nyah)(pah)(duh)(kwah)* . . . .
. . . . you're welcome, it's nothing
il y a *(eel-yah)* . . . . there is, there are
île, la *(eel)* . . . . island
ils *(eel)* . . . . they
imperméable, le *(a⁽ⁿ⁾-pair-may-ah-bluh)* . . . . raincoat
importance, la *(a⁽ⁿ⁾-por-tah⁽ⁿ⁾s)* . . . . importance
important (e) *(a⁽ⁿ⁾-por-tah⁽ⁿ⁾)* . . . . important
impossible *(a⁽ⁿ⁾-poh-see-bluh)* . . . . impossible
inacceptable *(een-ahk-sep-tah-bluh)* . . . . . . unacceptable
industrie, la *(a⁽ⁿ⁾-dew-stree)* . . . . industry
information, la *(a⁽ⁿ⁾-for-mah-syoh⁽ⁿ⁾)* . . . . information
ingénieur, le *(a⁽ⁿ⁾-zhay-nyur)* . . . . engineer
inscription, la *(a⁽ⁿ⁾-skreep-syoh⁽ⁿ⁾)* . . . . inscription
instant, le *(a⁽ⁿ⁾-stah⁽ⁿ⁾)* . . . . moment, instant
institut, le *(a⁽ⁿ⁾-stee-tew)* . . . . institute
interdit (e) *(a⁽ⁿ⁾-tair-dee)* . . . . prohibited
intéressant (e) *(a⁽ⁿ⁾-tay-ruh-sah⁽ⁿ⁾)* . . . . interesting
intérieur, le *(a⁽ⁿ⁾-tay-ree-ur)* . . . . . . domestic, inside, interior
interurbain (e) *(a⁽ⁿ⁾-tair-ewr-ba⁽ⁿ⁾)* . . . . long-distance
Irlande, la *(eer-lahnd)* . . . . Ireland
Israël, le *(ees-rah-el)* . . . . Israel
Italie, la *(ee-tah-lee)* . . . . Italy
italien (italienne) *(ee-tah-lya⁽ⁿ⁾)* . . . . Italian

J - K

jambon, le *(zhah⁽ⁿ⁾-boh⁽ⁿ⁾)* . . . . ham
janvier, le *(zhah⁽ⁿ⁾-vee-ay)* . . . . January
Japon, le *(zhah-poh⁽ⁿ⁾)* . . . . Japan
japonais (e) *(zhah-poh-nay)* . . . . Japanese
jaquette, la *(zhah-ket)* . . . . woman's jacket
jardin, le *(zhar-da⁽ⁿ⁾)* . . . . garden
jaune *(zhohn)* . . . . yellow
je *(zhuh)* I
jean, le *(jean)* . . . . jeans
jeudi, le *(zhuh-dee)* . . . . Thursday
jeune *(zhun)* . . . . young
jour, le *(zhoor)* . . . . day
journal, le *(zhoor-nahl)* . . . . newspaper
juif (juive) *(zhweef)* . . . . Jewish
juillet, le *(zhwee-ay)* . . . . July
juin, le *(zhwa⁽ⁿ⁾)* . . . . June
jupe, la *(zhewp)* . . . . skirt
jus, le *(zhoo)* . . . . juice
juste *(zhoost)* . . . . just, fair, right
justice, la *(zhoo-stees)* . . . . justice
kilo, le *(kee-loh)* . . . . kilo
kilomètre, le *(kee-loh-meh-truh)* . . . . kilometer
kiosque, le *(kee-ohsk)* . . . . news-stand, kiosk

L

l', la *(lah)* . . . . the (singular)
lac, le *(lack)* . . . . lake
lait, le *(lay)* . . . . milk
laiterie, la *(lay-tuh-ree)* . . . . dairy
lampe, la *(lahmp)* . . . . lamp
langue, la *(lah⁽ⁿ⁾-gwuh)* . . . . language
lavabo, le *(lah-vah-boh)* . . . . washbasin
laver *(lah-vay)* . . . . to wash
laverie automatique, la *(lah-vuh-ree)(oh-toh-mah-teek)* . . .
. . . . laundromat
le *(luh)* . . . . the (singular), it
leçon, la *(luh-soh⁽ⁿ⁾)* . . . . lesson
lecture, la *(lek-tewr)* . . . . reading
légume, le *(lay-gewm)* . . . . vegetable
lent (e) *(lah⁽ⁿ⁾)* . . . . slow
lentement *(lah⁽ⁿ⁾-tuh-mah⁽ⁿ⁾)* . . . . slowly

111

les *(lay)* .... the (plural)
lettre, la *(let-ruh)* .... letter
liberté, la *(lee-bair-tay)* .... liberty
librairie, la *(lee-brair-ree)* .... bookstore
libre *(lee-bruh)* .... free
lieu, le *(lyuh)* .... place
ligne, la *(leen-yuh)* .... line
limonade, la *(lee-moh-nahd)* .... lemonade
lire *(leer)* .... to read
liste, la *(leest)* .... list
lit, le *(lee)* .... bed
litre, le *(lee-truh)* .... liter
living-room, le *(lee-veeng-room)* .... living room
livre, le *(lee-vruh)* .... book
logement, le *(lohzh-mah(n))* ...... lodging, accommodation
long (longue) *(lohng)* .... long
louer *(loo-ay)* .... to rent
Louvre, le *(loo-vruh)* .... Louvre (museum)
lundi, le *(luh(n)-dee)* .... Monday
lunettes, les *(lew-net)* .... glasses
  lunettes de soleil, les *(lew-net)(duh)(soh-lay)* ... sunglasses
Luxembourg, le *(lewk-sah(n)-boor)* .... Luxembourg

M

Madame *(mah-dahm)* .... Mrs.
Mademoiselle *(mahd-mwah-zel)* .... Miss
magasin, le *(mah-gah-za(n))* .... store
  grand magasin, le *(grah(n))(mah-gah-za(n))* .. department store
magazine, le *(mah-gah-zeen)* .... magazine
magnifique *(mah-nee-feek)* .... magnificent
mai, le *(may)* .... May
maillot de bain, le *(my-oh)(duh)(ba(n))* ....
.... swimsuit, swim trunks
maillot de corps, le *(my-oh)(duh)(kor)* .... undershirt
maintenant *(ma(n)-tuh-nah(n))* .... now
mais *(may)* .... but
maison, la *(may-zoh(n))* .... house
mal *(mahl)* .... poorly, badly
malade *(mah-lahd)* .... sick
manger *(mah(n)-zhay)* .... to eat
manteau, le *(mah(n)-toh)* .... coat
marchand, le *(mar-shah(n))* .... merchant
marché, le *(mar-shay)* .... market
mardi, le *(mar-dee)* .... Tuesday
mariage, le *(mah-ree-ahzh)* ..... marriage, wedding
Maroc, le *(mah-rohk)* .... Morocco
marron *(mah-roh(n))* .... brown
mars, le *(marss)* .... March
matin, le *(mah-ta(n))* .... morning
mauvais (e) *(moh-vay)* .... bad
me *(muh)* .... to me
mécanicien, le *(may-kah-nee-sya(n))* .... mechanic
médecin, le *(may-duh-sa(n))* .... doctor
médicament, le *(may-dee-kah-mah(n))* .... medicine
mel, le *(mail)* .... email
menu, le *(muh-new)* .... menu
mer, la *(mair)* .... sea
merci *(mair-see)* .... thank you
mercredi, le *(mair-kruh-dee)* .... Wednesday
mère, la *(mair)* .... mother
messieurs, les *(mes-syur)* .... gentlemen
mètre, le *(meh-truh)* .... meter
métro, le *(may-troh)* .... subway
midi, le *(mee-dee)* .... noon
mille *(meel)* .... one thousand
minuit, le *(mee-nwee)* .... midnight
112 minute, la *(mee-newt)* .... minute

minuterie, la *(mee-new-tuh-ree)* .... automatic light switch
miroir, le *(mir-wahr)* .... mirror
mode, la *(mohd)* .... fashion
  à la mode *(ah)(lah)(mohd)* .... fashionable
moins *(mwa(n))* .... less
  moins le quart *(mwa(n))(luh)(kar)* .... a quarter to
mois, le *(mwah)* .... month
moment, le *(moh-mah(n))* .... moment
mon *(moh(n))* .... my
monde, le *(mohnd)* .... world
  tout le monde *(too)(luh)(mohnd)* .... everyone
monnaie, la *(moh-nay)* .... coins, money
Monsieur *(muh-syuh)* .... Mr.
montagne, la *(moh(n)-tahn-yuh)* .... mountain
montrer *(moh(n)-tray)* .... to show
mot, le *(moh)* .... word
moto, la *(moh-toh)* .... motorcycle
mots croisés, les *(moh)(kwah-zay)* .... crossword puzzle
mouchoir, le *(moo-shwahr)* .... handkerchief
mousse, la *(moos)* .... whipped cream, froth
moutarde, la *(moo-tard)* .... mustard
mouton, le *(moo-toh(n))* .... mutton
multicolore *(mewl-tee-koh-lor)* .... multi-colored
musée, le *(mew-zay)* .... museum
musique, la *(mew-zeek)* .... music
musulman (e) *(mew-zewl-mah(n))* .... Moslem

N

nation, la *(nah-syoh(n))* .... nation
nature, la *(nah-tewr)* .... nature
naturel (naturelle) *(nah-tew-rel)* .... natural
ne ... pas, n'... pas *(nuh)(pah)* .... no, not
ne ... rien *(nuh)(rya(n))* .... nothing
nécessaire *(nay-seh-sair)* .... necessary
nécessité, la *(nay-seh-see-tay)* .... necessity
neige (il neige) *(nehzh)* .... snow (it snows)
nettoyage à sec, le *(neh-twah-yahzh)(ah)(sek)* .. dry cleaner's
neuf *(nuf)* .... nine
neuf (neuve) *(nuf)* .... new
noir (e) *(nwahr)* .... black
nom, le *(noh(n))* .... name
nombre, le *(nohm-bruh)* .... number
non *(noh(n))* .... no
nord, le *(nor)* .... north
notre *(noh-truh)* .... our
nous *(noo)* .... we
nouveau (nouvelle) *(noo-voh)* .... new
novembre, le *(noh-vah(n)m-bruh)* .... November
nuit, la *(nwee)* .... night
numéro, le *(noo-may-roh)* .... number

O

objet, le *(ohb-zhay)* .... object
obligatoire *(oh-blee-gah-twahr)* ..... compulsory, obligatory
observation, la *(ohb-sair-vah-syoh(n))* .... observation
occupation, la *(oh-kew-pah-syoh(n))* .... occupation
occupé (e) *(oh-kew-pay)* .... busy, occupied
octobre, le *(ohk-toh-bruh)* .... October
odeur, la *(oh-dur)* .... smell
oeufs, les *(uh)* .... eggs
  oeuf à la coque *(uh)(ah)(lah)(kohk)* .... boiled egg
  oeufs brouillés *(uh)(broo-yay)* .... scrambled eggs
officiel (officielle) *(oh-fee-syel)* .... official
omelette, la *(ohm-let)* .... omelette
omnibus, le *(ohm-nee-boos)* .... slow train
on *(oh(n))* .... one, people, they, we
  on fait ça *(oh(n))(fay)(sah)* .... one does that

oncle, le *(oh(n)-kluh)*	uncle
ont *(oh(n))*	(they) have
onze *(oh(n)z)*	eleven
opéra, le *(oh-peh-rah)*	opera
opérateur, le *(oh-peh-rah-tur)*	operator
optimiste, le *(ohp-tee-meest)*	optimist
orange, la *(oh-rah(n)zh)*	orange (color)
orchestre, le *(or-kess-truh)*	orchestra
ordinaire *(or-dee-nair)*	ordinary
ordinateur, le *(or-dee-nah-tur)*	computer
oreiller, le *(oh-ray-yay)*	pillow
organisé (e) *(or-gah-nee-zay)*	organized
Orient, le *(oh-ree-ah(n))*	Orient
original (e) *(oh-ree-zhee-nahl)*	original
origine, la *(oh-ree-zheen)*	origin
ou *(oo)*	or
où *(oo)*	where
oublier *(oo-blee-ay)*	to forget
ouest, le *(west)*	west
oui *(wee)*	yes
ouvert (e) *(oo-vair)*	open
ouvrez *(oo-vray)*	open!

P

page, la *(pahzh)*	page
pain, le *(pa(n))*	bread
paire, la *(pair)*	pair
pantalon, le *(pah(n)-tah-loh(n))*	trousers
pantoufle, la *(pah(n)-too-fluh)*	slipper
Pape, le *(pahp)*	Pope
papeterie, la *(pah-peh-tuh-ree)*	stationery store
papier, le *(pah-pee-ay)*	paper
paquet, le *(pah-kay)*	package
par *(par)*	by, per
par avion *(par)(ah-vyoh(n))*	by airmail
parapluie, le *(pah-rah-plew-ee)*	umbrella
parc, le *(park)*	park
pardon *(par-doh(n))*	excuse me
parent, le *(pah-rah(n))*	parent, relative
parfait (e) *(par-fay)*	perfect
parfum, le *(par-fuh(n))*	perfume
parfumerie, la *(par-few-muh-ree)*	perfumery
parking, le *(par-keeng)*	parking lot
parler *(par-lay)*	to speak
partir *(par-teer)*	to leave, depart
passeport, le *(pahs-por)*	passport
pâtisserie, la *(pah-tee-suh-ree)*	pastry, pastry shop
pauvre *(poh-vruh)*	poor
payer *(pay-yay)*	to pay
Pays-Bas, les *(pay-ee-bah)*	Netherlands
peigne, le *(pen-yuh?)*	comb
pellicule, la *(peh-lee-kewl)*	film
pendule, la *(pah(n)-dewl)*	clock
perdre *(pair-druh)*	to lose
père, le *(pair)*	father
personne, la *(pair-sohn)*	person
petit (e) *(puh-tee)*	small
petit-déjeuner, le *(puh-tee-day-zhuh-nay)*	breakfast
peu, un *(puh)*	a little
peuple, le *(puh-pluh)*	people
pharmacie, la *(far-mah-see)*	pharmacy
photo, la *(foh-toh)*	photo, photograph
phrase, la *(frahz)*	sentence
pièce, la *(pyess)*	room, piece
pilule, la *(pee-lewl)*	pill
pique-nique, le *(peek-neek)*	picnic
placard, le *(plah-kar)*	cupboard, closet

place, la *(plahs)*	seat, place, square (in a town)
plaisir, le *(play-zeer)*	pleasure
avec plaisir *(avek)(play-zeer)*	with pleasure
plan, le *(plah(n))*	map
plat du jour, le *(plah)(dew)(zhoor)*	daily special
pleut (il pleut) *(pluh)*	rain (it rains)
plus *(plew)*	more
poisson, le *(pwah-soh(n))*	fish
poissonnerie, la *(pwah-soh(n)-nuh-ree)*	fish shop
poivre, le *(pwah-vruh)*	pepper
Pôle nord, le *(pohl)(nor)*	North Pole
Pôle sud, le *(pohl)(sood)*	South Pole
police, la *(poh-lees)*	police
politesse, la *(poh-lee-tess)*	politeness
politique, la *(poh-lee-teek)*	politics
pomme, la *(pohm)*	apple
pont, le *(poh(n))*	bridge
porc, le *(por)*	pork
port, le *(por)*	port
porte, la *(port)*	door, gate
portefeuille, le *(port-fuh-yuh)*	wallet
porteur, le *(por-tur)*	porter
Portugal, le *(por-too-gahl)*	Portugal
poste, la *(pohst)*	mail, post office
poste de police, le *(pohst)(duh)(poh-lees)*	police station
potage, le *(poh-tahzh)*	soup
poulet, le *(poo-lay)*	chicken
pour *(poor)*	for
pourboire, le *(poor-bwahr)*	tip
pourquoi *(poor-kwah)*	why
pousser *(poo-say)*	to push
pouvoir *(poo-vwahr)*	to be able to, can
premier (première) *(pruh-mee-air)*	first
prendre *(prah(n)-druh)*	to take
prendre l'avion *(prah(n)-druh)(lah-vyoh(n))*	to fly, to take the plane
préposition, la *(pray-poh-zee-syoh(n))*	preposition
président, le *(pray-zee-dah(n))*	president
presse, la *(press)*	press, media
printemps, le *(prah(n)-tah(n))*	spring
prix, le *(pree)*	price
problème, le *(proh-blem)*	problem
programme, la *(proh-grahm)*	program
propre *(proh-pruh)*	clean
protestant (e) *(proh-teh-stah(n))*	Protestant
pull, le *(pul)*	sweater
pyjama, le *(pee-zhah-mah)*	pajamas

Q

qu' *(kuh)*	what, that
Qu'est-ce que c'est? *(kess)(kuh)(say)*	What is it?
quai, le *(kay)*	platform
quand *(kah(n))*	when
quarante *(kah-rah(n)t)*	forty
quart, le *(kar)*	a quarter
et quart *(ay)(kar)*	a quarter past
quartier, le *(kar-tee-ay)*	quarter, district
quatorze *(kah-torz)*	fourteen
quatre *(kah-truh)*	four
quatre-vingt-dix *(kah-truh-va(n)-deess)*	ninety
quatre-vingts *(kah-truh-va(n))*	eighty
que *(kuh)*	what, that
Québec *(kay-bek)*	Quebec (Canada)
quel *(kel)*	what, which
quelle *(kel)*	what, which
question, la *(kes-tyoh(n))*	question
qui *(key)*	who, what

quinze (ka$^{(n)}$z) . . . . fifteen
quoi (kwah) . . . . what

R

raisin, le (ray-za$^{(n)}$) . . . . grape
raisin sec, le (ray-za$^{(n)}$)(sek) . . . . raisin
rapide (rah-peed) . . . . fast
rapide, le (rah-peed) . . . . (fast) train
rasoir, le (rah-zwahr) . . . . razor
recette, la (ruh-set) . . . . recipe
récréation, la (ray-kray-ah-syoh$^{(n)}$) . . . . . recreation, recess
réfrigérateur, le (ray-free-zhay-rah-tuhr) . . . . . refrigerator
région, la (ray-zhoh$^{(n)}$) . . . . region, area
religion, la (ruh-lee-zhoh$^{(n)}$) . . . . religion
Renaissance, la (ruh-nay-sah$^{(n)}$s) . . rebirth, the Renaissance
rendez-vous, le (rah$^{(n)}$-day-voo) . . . . date, appointment
repas, le (ruh-pah) . . . . meal
répéter (ray-pay-tay) . . . . to repeat
répétez (ray-pay-tay) . . . . repeat!
réponse, la (ray-poh$^{(n)}$s) . . . . answer
république, la (ray-pew-bleek) . . . . republic
RER (air-uh-air) . . . . transportation network (in Paris)
réservation, la (ray-zair-vah-syoh$^{(n)}$) . . . . . reservation
réserver (ray-zair-vay) . . . . to reserve, to book
résidence, la (ray-zee-dah$^{(n)}$s) . . . . residence
résistance, la (ray-zee-stah$^{(n)}$s) . . . . resistance
restaurant, le (reh-stoh-rah$^{(n)}$) . . . . restaurant
reste, le (rehst) . . . . rest, remaining
rester (reh-stay) . . . . to remain, stay
réveil, le (ray-vay) . . . . alarm clock
révolution, la (ray-voh-lew-syoh$^{(n)}$) . . . . revolution
revue, la (ruh-vew) . . . . magazine
rez-de-chaussée, le (ray-duh-shoh-say) . . . . . . ground floor
riche (reesh) . . . . rich
rideau, le (ree-doh) . . . . curtain
rien (rya$^{(n)}$) . . . . nothing
robe, la (rohb) . . . . dress
robe de chambre, la (rohb)(duh)(shah$^{(n)}$-bruh) . . . . bathrobe
rose (rohz) . . . . pink
rôti (e) (roh-tee) . . . . roasted
rouge (roozh) . . . . red
route, la (root) . . . . highway, road
rue, la (rew) . . . . street
russe (roos) . . . . Russian
Russie, la (roo-see) . . . . Russia

S

sac, le (sack) . . . . bag, sack
sac à main, le (sahk)(ah)(mah$^{(n)}$) . . . . handbag
sacré (sah-kray) . . . . sacred
sage (sahzh) . . . . wise, well-behaved
saison, la (say-zoh$^{(n)}$) . . . . season
salade, la (sah-lahd) . . . . salad
salle à manger, la (sahl)(ah)(mah$^{(n)}$-zhay) . . . . dining room
salle d'attente, la (sahl)(dah-tah$^{(n)}$t) . . . . waiting room
salle de bains, la (sahl)(duh)(ba$^{(n)}$) . . . . bathroom
salon, le (sah-loh$^{(n)}$) . . . . living room
salut (sah-lew) . . . . hello, hi
salutations, les (sah-lew-tah-syoh$^{(n)}$) . . . . greeting
samedi, le (sahm-dee) . . . . Saturday
sandale, la (sah$^{(n)}$-dahl) . . . . sandal
sandwich, le (sah$^{(n)}$-dweech) . . . . sandwich
sans (sah$^{(n)}$) . . . . without
santé, la (sah$^{(n)}$-tay) . . . . health
en bonne santé (ah$^{(n)}$)(bun)(sah$^{(n)}$-tay) . . . . . healthy
sauce, la (sohs) . . . . sauce
saumon, le (soh-moh$^{(n)}$) . . . . salmon

savoir (sah-vwahr) . . . . to know
savon, le (sah-voh$^{(n)}$) . . . . soap
science, la (see-ah$^{(n)}$s) . . . . science
second (e) (suh-goh$^{(n)}$d) . . . . second
second, la (seh-goh$^{(n)}$d) . . . . second (time)
secours, le (suh-koor) . . . . help
au secours (oh)(suh-koor) . . . . help!
secrétaire, le/la (suh-kray-tair) . . . . secretary
sécurité, la (say-kew-ree-tay) . . . . security
seize (sehz) . . . . sixteen
sel, le (sel) . . . . salt
semaine, la (suh-men) . . . . week
sentiment, le (sah$^{(n)}$-tee-mah$^{(n)}$) . . . . feeling
sept (set) . . . . seven
septembre, le (sep-tah$^{(n)}$m-bruh) . . . . September
serons (sair-oh$^{(n)}$) . . . . (we) will be
serveur, le (sair-vur) . . . . waiter
serveuse, la (sair-vuz) . . . . waitress
service, le (sair-vees) . . . . service
serviette, la (sair-vyet) . . . . napkin, towel
short, le (short) . . . . shorts
s'il vous plaît (seel)(voo)(play) . . . . please
similarité, la (see-mee-lar-ee-tay) . . . . similarity
situation, la (see-tew-ah-syoh$^{(n)}$) . . . . situation
six (seess) . . . . six
ski, le (skee) . . . . skiing
ski-nautique, le (skee-noh-teek) . . . . . . water skiing
slip, le (sleep) . . . . underpants
soeur, la (suhr) . . . . sister
soif, la (swahf) . . . . thirst
soir, le (swahr) . . . . evening
soixante (swah-sah$^{(n)}$t) . . . . sixty
soixante-dix (swah-sah$^{(n)}$t-deess) . . . . seventy
soleil, le (soh-lay) . . . . sun
somme, la (sohm) . . . . sum
sommes (sohm) . . . . (we) are
sont (soh$^{(n)}$) . . . . (they) are
Sorbonne, la (sor-bun) . . . . part of University of Paris
sortie, la (sor-tee) . . . . exit
sortir (sor-teer) . . . . to go out, leave, exit
soupe, la (soup) . . . . soup
sous (soo) . . . . under
sous-sol, le (soo-sohl) . . . . basement
soutien-gorge, le (soo-tya$^{(n)}$-gorzh) . . . . brassiere
souvenir, le (soo-vuh-neer) . . . . souvenir
spectacle, le (spek-tah-kluh) . . . . . . spectacle, performance
sport, le (spor) . . . . sport
station d'essence, la (stah-syoh$^{(n)}$)(day-sah$^{(n)}$s) . . gas station
station de métro, la (stah-syoh$^{(n)}$)(duh)(may-troh) . . . .
. . . . subway station
stop, le (stohp) . . . . stop
stopper (stoh-pay) . . . . to stop
stupide (stew-peed) . . . . stupid
stylo, le (stee-loh) . . . . pen
sucre, le (soo-kruh) . . . . sugar
sud, le (sood) . . . . south
Suède, la (swed) . . . . Sweden
suis (swee) . . . . (I) am
Suisse, la (swees) . . . . Switzerland
suivant (e) (swee-vah$^{(n)}$) . . . . following
supérieur (e) (syoo-pay-ree-ur) . . . . superior, upper
supermarché, le (soo-pair-mar-shay) . . . . . . supermarket
sur (sewr) . . . . on
sûr (e) (sur) . . . . sure, certain
surprise, la (sewr-preez) . . . . surprise
sympathique (sa$^{(n)}$-pah-teek) . . . . likeable, nice
système, le (see-stem) . . . . system

T

tabac, le *(tah-bah)* . . . . tobacco
table, la *(tah-bluh)* . . . . table
tableau, le *(tah-bloh)* . . . . picture
taille, la *(tie)* . . . . size (clothing)
tante, la *(taunt)* . . . . aunt
tapis, le *(tah-pee)* . . . . carpet
tapisserie, la *(tah-pee-suh-ree)* . . . . tapestry, wallpaper
tarif, le *(tah-reef)* . . . . price, tariff, fare
tasse, la *(tahs)* . . . . cup
taxe, la *(tahx)* . . . . tax, charge
taxi, le *(tahx-ee)* . . . . taxi
teeshirt, le *(tee-shirt)* . . . . T-shirt
télécarte, la *(tay-lay-kart)* . . . . telephone card
téléphone, le *(tay-lay-fohn)* . . . . telephone
téléphoner *(tay-lay-foh-nay)* . . . . to telephone
télévision, la *(tay-lay-vee-syoh(n))* . . . . television
température, la *(tah(n)-pay-rah-tewr)* . . . . temperature
temps, le *(tah(n))* . . . . weather, time
tennis, le *(teh-nees)* . . . . tennis
tennis, les *(teh-nees)* . . . . tennis shoes
terrasse, la *(tay-rahs)* . . . . terrace, sidewalk (café)
thé, le *(tay)* . . . . tea
théâtre, le *(tay-ah-truh)* . . . . theater
thermal (e) *(tair-mahl)* . . . . thermal
thermomètre, le *(tair-moh-meh-truh)* . . . . thermometer
ticket, le *(tee-kay)* . . . . ticket
timbre, le *(ta(n)-bruh)* . . . . stamp
tirer *(tee-ray)* . . . . to pull
toilettes, les *(twah-let)* . . . . toilets
toujours *(too-zhoor)* . . . . always
tour, la *(tour)* . . . . tower
tour, le *(tour)* . . . . tour, circumference
tourner *(toor-nay)* . . . . to turn
tout *(too)* . . . . everything
tout droit *(too)(dwah)* . . . . straight ahead
train, le *(tra(n))* . . . . train
transport, le *(trah(n)-spor)* . . . . transportation
treize *(trehz)* . . . . thirteen
trente *(trah(n)t)* . . . . thirty
très *(treh)* . . . . very
tricolore *(tree-koh-lor)* . . . . tricolored
trois *(twah)* . . . . three
troisième *(twah-zee-em)* . . . . third
trop cher *(troh)(shair)* . . . . too expensive
trouver *(troo-vay)* . . . . to find
tu *(too)* . . . . you (singular/informal)
Tunisie, la *(tew-nee-zee)* . . . . Tunisia
typique *(tee-peek)* . . . . typical

U

un *(uh(n))* . . . . a, one (masculine)
une *(ewn)* . . . . a, one (feminine)
unique *(ew-neek)* . . . . sole, only, single
universel *(ew-nee-vair-sel)* . . . . universal
université, la *(ew-nee-vair-see-tay)* . . . . university
urgence, la *(ewr-zhah(n)s)* . . . . urgency, emergency
utilisez *(oo-tee-lee-zay)* . . . . use!

V

vacances, les *(vah-kah(n)s)* . . . . vacation, holiday
vais *(vay)* . . . . (I) go
valise, la *(vah-leez)* . . . . suitcase
valse, la *(vahls)* . . . . waltz
vanille, la *(vah-nee-yuh)* . . . . vanilla
variété, la *(vah-ree-ay-tay)* . . . . variety
veau, le *(voh)* . . . . veal

veine, la *(ven)* . . . . vein (in the body)
vélo, le *(vay-loh)* . . . . bicycle
vendre *(vah(n)-druh)* . . . . to sell
vendredi *(vah(n)-druh-dee)* . . . . Friday
venir *(vuh-neer)* . . . . to come
vent, le *(vah(n))* . . . . wind
vente, la *(vah(n)t)* . . . . sale
verbe, le *(vairb)* . . . . verb
verre, le *(vair)* . . . . glass
verre à vin, le *(vair)(ah)(va(n))* . . . . . wine glass
version, la *(vair-syoh(n))* . . . . version
vert (e) *(vair)* . . . . green
veston, le *(veh-stoh(n))* . . . . jacket, blazer
vêtement, le *(vet-mah(n))* . . . . clothes
viande, la *(vee-ah(n)d)* . . . . meat
vie, la *(vee)* . . . . life
vierge, la *(vee-airzh)* . . . . virgin
vieux (vieille) *(vee-yuh)* . . . . old
vigne, la *(veen-yuh)* . . . . grape vine
vigneron, le *(veen-yur-oh(n))* . . . . . . wine-grower
vignoble, le *(veen-yoh-bluh)* . . . . vineyard
village, le *(vee-lahzh)* . . . . village
ville, la *(vee)* . . . . city
vin, le *(va(n))* . . . . wine
vingt *(va(n))* . . . . twenty
violet (violette) *(vee-oh-lay)* . . . . violet
visite, la *(vee-zeet)* . . . . visit
visiter *(vee-zee-tay)* . . . . to visit
vitamine, la *(vee-tah-meen)* . . . . vitamin
vocabulaire, le *(voh-kah-bew-lair)* . . . . vocabulary
voilà *(vwah-lah)* . . . . there is, there are
voir *(vwahr)* . . . . to see
voiture, la *(vwah-tewr)* . . . . car
voiture de location, la *(vwah-tewr)(duh)(loh-kah-syoh(n))* . .
. . . . rental car
vol, le *(vohl)* . . . . flight
volaille, la *(voh-lie)* . . . . poultry
vos *(voh)* . . . . your
votre *(voh-truh)* . . . . your
vouloir *(voo-lwahr)* . . . . to want
je veux *(zhuh)(vuh)* . . . . I want
je voudrais *(zhuh)(voo-dray)* . . . . I would like
vous voulez *(voo)(voo-lay)* . . . . you want
vous *(voo)* . . . . you (singular and plural)
vous *(voo)* . . . . to you
voyage, le *(vwah-yahzh)* . . . . trip, travel
Bon voyage! *(boh(n))(vwah-yahzh)* . . . . . . have a good trip
voyager *(vwah-yah-zhay)* . . . . to travel
voyager en avion *(vwah-yah-zhay)(ah(n))(ah-vyoh(n))* . . to fly
voyageur, le *(vwah-yah-zhur)* . . . . traveler

W - Y - Z

W.C., le *(doo-bul-vay-say)* . . . . water closet, toilet
wagon, le *(vah-goh(n))* . . . . railroad car
wagon-lit, le *(vah-goh(n)-lee)* . . . . sleeping car
wagon-restaurant, le *(vah-goh(n)-reh-stoh-rah(n))* . . dining car
week-end, le *(week-end)* . . . . weekend
western, le *(wes-tairn)* . . . . western (film)
whisky, le *(wee-skee)* . . . . whisky
y a-t-il *(yah-teel)* . . . . are there? is there?
zèle, le *(zel)* . . . . zeal, ardor
zénith, le *(zay-neet)* . . . . zenith, peak
zéphyr, le *(zay-feer)* . . . . balmy breeze
zéro *(zay-roh)* . . . . zero
zodiaque, le *(zoh-dee-ahk)* . . . . zodiac
zone de silence, la *(zohn)(duh)(see-lah(n)s)* . . . . . quiet zone
zoo, le *(zoh)* . . . . zoo
zoologie, la *(zoh-oh-loh-zhee)* . . . . zoology
zut! *(zewt)* . . . . rats! darn!

This beverage guide is intended to explain the variety of beverages available to you while **en France ou** any other French-speaking country. It is by no means complete. Some of the experimenting has been left up to you, but this should get you started.

BOISSONS CHAUDES (hot drinks)

café noir	coffee, black
café au lait	coffee with milk
café crème	coffee with cream
café express	espresso
café filtre	filtered coffee

chocolat	cocoa
thé	tea
thé au citron	tea with lemon
thé au lait	tea with milk

BOISSONS FROIDES (cold drinks)

lait froid	cold milk
lait aromatisé	flavored milk
eau minérale	mineral water
jus de fruits	fruit juice
jus d'orange	orange juice
jus de pomme	apple juice
jus de tomate	tomato juice
orange pressée	fresh squeezed orange juice
thé glacé	iced tea
café glacé	iced coffee
les glaçons	ice cubes

BIÈRES (beer)
There are a variety of brands including both **blonde** (light) and **brune** (dark). **La bière** is purchased **en bouteille** (bottle) or **à la pression** (draught).

VINS (wine)
Wine production in France is closely controlled by the government, making it much easier to know what you are buying. You may drink wine by the **verre** (glass), the **carafe** (carafe) or the **bouteille** (bottle).

vin rouge	red wine
vin blanc	white wine
vin rosé	rosé wine
vin mousseux	sparkling wine
vin ordinaire	table wine
vin de table	table wine
vin de la maison	the "house" wine
vin du pays	local wine of the region

A.O.C. (Appelation d'origine contrôlée)
superior wine
V.D.Q.S. (Vins délimités de qualité supérieure)
choice wine
Premier cru/Grand cru
good vintage wine

APÉRITIFS (aperitifs)
These may be enjoyed straight or over ice.

porto	port
Pastis	aniseed-flavored aperitif
Pineau des Charentes	grape juice and cognac
Kir	Crème de Cassis and white wine

ALCOOL (spirits)
Cocktail drinking is not widespread in France. The following are available in large, international hotels and "**Bars américains.**"

gin	gin
vodka	vodka
rhum	rum
whisky	scotch
bourbon	bourbon
martini dry	American maritini

CUT ALONG THIS DOTTED LINE, FOLD AND TAKE WITH YOU

La Carte
menu

FOLD HERE

FOLD HERE

Salades (salads)

laitue	lettuce salad
chicorée	chicory
escarole	coarse-leafed green lettuce
endive belge	Belgian endive
mâche	wild field lettuce
romaine	romaine
mimosa	green salad with egg yolks
mixte	mixed
niçoise	string beans, potatoes, and tuna
verte	tossed green
de saison	seasonal
de tomates	tomato
vinaigrette	in vinegar and oil

Légumes (vegetables)

haricots verts	green string beans
flageolets	small, pale green beans
petits pois	peas
lentilles	lentils
asperges	asparagus
carottes	carrots
épinards	spinach
poireaux	leeks
tomates	tomatoes
champignons	cultivated mushrooms
chanterelles	wild mushrooms
morilles	morel, wild mushrooms
chou	cabbage
chou-fleur	cauliflower
choux de Bruxelles	brussels sprouts
betteraves	beets
maïs	corn
concombres	cucumbers
navets	turnips
oignons	onions
radis	radishes
ail	garlic
artichauts	artichoke
aubergines	eggplant
courgettes	zucchini squash

Pommes de terre (potatoes)

croquettes	mashed, breaded and fried
gratin dauphinois	scalloped
frites	French-fried
à l'anglaise	peeled and boiled
nature	plain boiled
maître d'hôtel	boiled and sautéed
purée	mashed
vapeur	steamed

Fruit (fruit)

pomme	apple
poire	pear
abricot	apricot
pêche	peach
banane	banana
orange	orange
mandarine	mandarin orange
cerise	cherry
prune	plum
pruneau	prune
melon	melon
pamplemousse	grapefruit
pastèque	watermelon
raisin	grape
raisin sec	raisin
grenade	pomegranate
ananas	pineapple
citron	lemon
compote de fruits	stewed fruits

Baies (berries)

fraise	strawberry
framboise	raspberry
mûre	blackberry
cassis	black currant
myrtille	bilberry
airelle	blueberry
groseille	red currant

Préparation (preparation)

cuit	cooked
cru	raw
rôti	roasted
frit	fried
cuit au four	baked
grillé	grilled
farci	stuffed or filled
bouilli	boiled
fumé	smoked
mariné	marinated
braisé	braised
en croûte	cooked in pastry crust
gratiné	sprinkled with cheese
au jus	cooked in its own juice
bleu	extremely rare
saignant	rare
à point	medium rare
bien cuit	well done

Autres (others)

confiture	jam
miel	honey
huile	oil
vinaigre	vinegar
moutarde	mustard
riz	rice
nouilles	noodles
pâtes	pasta
fromage	cheese
gâteau	cake
pâtisserie	pastry
glace	ice cream
chantilly	whipped cream
yaourt	yoghurt

(boh⁽ⁿ⁾) (nah-pay-tee)
Bon appétit!
enjoy your meal

Viande (meat)

Veau (veal)

blanquette de veau	veal stew with gravy
côte de veau	veal chop
côtelette de veau	veal chop
foie de veau	calf's liver
fricassée de veau	veal stew
médaillons de veau	medallions of pan-fried veal
tête de veau	head of veal
escalope de veau	veal cutlet
tendron de veau	braised breast of veal
rognons de veau	veal kidneys
ris de veau	veal sweetbreads
poitrine de veau farcie	stuffed breast of veal
noisette de veau	tenderloin morsels of veal

Agneau (lamb)

carré d'agneau	lamb rib roast
côte/côtelette	lamb chop
épaule d'agneau	lamb shoulder
gigot d'agneau	leg of lamb

Volaille (poultry)

poulet	chicken
coq au vin	chicken in wine sauce
canard	duck
caneton	duckling
chapon	capon
caille	quail
oie	goose
faisan	pheasant
dinde	turkey

Gibier (wild game)

gigue de chevreuil	roast leg of venison
bécasse	woodcock
escalope de sanglier	cutlets of wild boar
cuissot de marcassin	roast leg of wild pig
râble de lapin	saddle of rabbit

FOLD HERE

Boeuf (beef)

boeuf bourguignon	red wine stew
carbonades de boeuf	sautéed and braised slices
côte de boeuf	beef rib steaks
entrecôte de boeuf	boneless beef rib steak
estouffade de boeuf	braised beef in wine stew
filet de boeuf	tenderloin of beef
médaillon de boeuf	thick discs of tenderloin
queue de boeuf	oxtail
tournedos	beef tenderloin
terrine de boeuf	casserole stew
tripes	stomach lining
moelle	beef bone marrow

Porc (pork)

côte/côtelette	pork chop
carré de porc provençal	rib loin roast with spices
cuissot de porc	fresh ham roast
jarret de porc	pork shank
pied de porc	pig's foot
rognons de porc	pork kidneys
rôti de porc	pork roast

Poissons et fruits de mer (fish and seafood)

anchois	anchovies
anguille	eel
cabillaud	codfish
calamar	squid
carpe	carp
colin	hake
coquillages	shellfish
coquilles Saint-Jacques	scallops
crabe	crab
crevettes	shrimps
écrevisses	fresh-water crayfish
flétan	halibut
grenouille	frog
hareng	herring
homard	lobster; with claws
langouste	spiny lobster; no claws
langoustine	shellfish
moules	mussels
perche	perch
poulpe	small octopus
saumon	salmon
sole	sole
truite	trout
thon	tuna

FOLD HERE

Hors-d'oeuvre (appetizers)

huîtres	oysters
assiette de charcuterie	assorted sausages, salamis
crudités	raw vegetables
escargots	snails
foie gras truffé	goose liver with truffles
jambon cru	raw-cured ham
pâté de campagne	country style, course pâté
salade panachée	mixed vegetable salad
terrine maison	house pâté in terrine
croque-monsieur	grilled ham and cheese sandwich
croque-madame	grilled chicken and cheese sandwich

Potages (soups)

bisque	cream soup with seafood
bouillabaisse	rich fish soup
crème de tomates	cream of tomato
pistou	vegetable soup
soupe du jour	soup of the day
soupe à l'oignon	onion soup
consommé	clarified stock
soupe à la reine	chicken soup with rice
velouté de légumes	thick vegetable soup
vichyssoise	potato and leek soup

Oeufs (eggs)

à la coque	soft-boiled
mollets	medium-boiled
brouillés	scrambled
durs	hard-boiled
pochés	poached
omelette nature	plain omelette
omelette au fromage	cheese omelette
quiche	cheese and egg pie

(zhuh)
je

(noo)
nous

(eel)
il

(voo)
vous

(el)
elle

(eel) *(el)*
ils/elles

(par-lay)
parler
(parl)
je parle

(ah-bee-tay)
habiter
(zhah-beet)
j'habite

(ah-shuh-tay)
acheter
(zhah-shet)
j'achète

(reh-stay)
rester
(rest)
je reste

(koh-mah(n)-day)
commander
(koh-mah(n)d)
je commande

(sah-puh-lay)
s'appeler
(mah-pel)
je m'appelle

we	I
you	he
they (♂) / they (♀)	she
to live/reside	to speak
I live/reside	I speak
to remain/stay	to buy
I remain/stay	I buy
to be called	to order
I am called/my name is . . .	I order

(vuh-neer)
venir
(vyah^{(n)})
je viens

(ah-lay)
aller
(vay)
je vais

(ah-prah^{(n)}-druh)
apprendre
(zhah-prah^{(n)})
j'apprends

(ah-vwahr)
avoir
(zhay)
j'ai

(voo-dray)
je voudrais

(ah-vwahr)   *(buh-zwa^{(n)})*   *(duh)*
avoir besoin de
(zhay)   *(buh-zwa^{(n)})*   *(duh)*
j'ai besoin de

(mah^{(n)}-zhay)
manger
(mah^{(n)}zh)
je mange

(bwahr)
boire
(bwah)
je bois

(deer)
dire
(dee)
je dis

(vah^{(n)}-druh)
vendre
(vah^{(n)})
je vends

(koh^{(n)}-prah^{(n)}-druh)
comprendre
(koh^{(n)}-prah^{(n)})
je comprends

(ray-pay-tay)
répéter
(ray-pet)
je répète

to go	to come
I go	I come
to have	to learn
I have	I learn
to need	
I need	I would like
to drink	to eat
I drink	I eat
to sell	to say
I sell	I say
to repeat	to understand
I repeat	I understand

(shair-shay)
chercher
(shairsh)
je cherche

(vwahr)
voir
(vwah)
je vois

(ah⁽ⁿ⁾-vwah-yay)
envoyer
(zhah⁽ⁿ⁾-vwah)
j'envoie

(dor-meer)
dormir
(dor)
je dors

(fair)
faire
(fay)
je fais

(pay-yay)
payer
(pay)
je paie

(moh⁽ⁿ⁾-tray)
montrer
(moh⁽ⁿ⁾-truh)
je montre

(ay-kreer)
écrire
(zhay-kree)
j'écris

(leer)
lire
(lee)
je lis

(poo-vwahr)
pouvoir
(puh)
je peux

(duh-vwahr)
devoir
(dwah)
je dois

(sah-vwahr)
savoir
(say)
je sais

to see	to look for
I see	I look for
to sleep	to send
I sleep	I send
to pay	to make/do
I pay	I make/do
to write	to show
I write	I show
to be able to/can	to read
I can	I read
to know	to have to/must
I know	I have to/must

(sor-teer)
sortir

(sor)
je sors

(prah⁽ⁿ⁾-druh) *(lah-vyoh⁽ⁿ⁾)*
prendre l'avion

(prah⁽ⁿ⁾) *(lah-vyoh⁽ⁿ⁾)*
je prends l'avion

(vwah-yah-zhay)
voyager

(vwah-yahzh)
je voyage

(par-teer)
partir

(tra⁽ⁿ⁾) *(par)*
le train part

(ah-ree-vay)
arriver

(zhah-reev)
j'arrive

(shah⁽ⁿ⁾-zhay) *(duh)* *(tra⁽ⁿ⁾)*
changer de train

(shah⁽ⁿ⁾zh) *(tra⁽ⁿ⁾)*
je change de train

(fair) *(lay)* *(vah-leez)*
faire les valises

(fay) *(vah-leez)*
je fais les valises

(lah-vay)
laver

(lahv)
je lave

(eel-yah)
il y a

(eel) *(foh)*
il faut . . .

(doh⁽ⁿ⁾-nay-mwah)
donnez-moi . . .

(pair-druh)
perdre

(pair)
je perds

to fly / take the plane

I fly

to leave / go out

I leave

to leave / depart

the train leaves

to travel

I travel

to transfer (trains)

I transfer trains

to arrive

I arrive

to wash

I wash

to pack

I pack

it is necessary . . .

there is/there are

to lose

I lose

give me . . .

(oh-zhoor-dwee)
aujourd'hui

(koh-mah⁽ⁿ⁾)   *(tah-lay-voo)*
Comment allez-vous?

(ee-air)
hier

(seel)   *(voo)*   *(play)*
s'il vous plaît

(duh-ma⁽ⁿ⁾)
demain

(mair-see)
merci

(oh)   *(ruh-vwahr)*
au revoir

(par-doh⁽ⁿ⁾)
pardon

(ah⁽ⁿ⁾-syah⁽ⁿ⁾)   *(noo-voh)*
ancien - nouveau

(kohm-bya⁽ⁿ⁾)   *(sah)*   *(koot)*
Combien ça coûte?

(grah⁽ⁿ⁾)   *(puh-tee)*
grand - petit

(oo-vair)   *(fair-may)*
ouvert - fermé

How are you?   today

please   yesterday

thank you   tomorrow

excuse me   goodbye

How much does
that cost?   old   -   new

open   -   closed   large   -   small

(ah⁽ⁿ⁾) *(bun)* *(sah⁽ⁿ⁾-tay)* *(mah-lahd)*
en bonne santé - malade

(boh⁽ⁿ⁾) *(moh-vay)*
bon - mauvais

(shoh) *(fwah)*
chaud - froid

(koor) *(lohng)*
court - long

(oh) *(bah)*
haut - bas

(ah⁽ⁿ⁾) *(oh)* *(ah⁽ⁿ⁾)* *(bah)*
en haut - en bas

(gohsh) *(dwaht)*
gauche - droite

(lah⁽ⁿ⁾) *(rah-peed)*
lent - rapide

(vee-yuh) *(zhun)*
vieux - jeune

(shair) *(boh⁽ⁿ⁾)* *(mar-shay)*
cher - bon marché

(poh-vruh) *(reesh)*
pauvre - riche

(boh-koo) *(oon)* *(puh)*
beaucoup - un peu

good - bad	healthy - sick
short - long	hot - cold
above - below	high - low
slow - fast	left - right
expensive- inexpensive	old - young
a lot - a little	poor - rich

Now that you've finished...

You've done it!

You've completed all the Steps, stuck your labels, flashed your cards and cut out your menu guide. Do you realize how far you've come and how much you've learned?

You can now confidently

- ask questions,
- understand directions,
- make reservations,
- order food and
- shop anywhere.

And you can do it all in a foreign language! You can now go anywhere — from a large cosmopolitan restaurant to a small, out-of-the-way village where no one speaks English. Your experiences will be much more enjoyable and worry-free now that you speak the language.

Yes, learning a foreign language can be fun.

Kristine Kershul

Send us this order form with your check, money order or credit card details. If paying by credit card, you may fax your order to **(206) 284-3660** or call us toll-free at **(800) 488-5068**. All prices are in US dollars and are subject to change without notice.

* What about shipping costs?

STANDARD DELIVERY per address

If your items total	please add
up to $ 20.00	$5.00
$20.01 - $ 40.00	$6.00
$40.01 - $ 60.00	$7.00
$60.01 - $ 80.00	$8.00
$80.01 - $ 100.00	$9.00

If over $100, please call for charges.

For shipping outside the U.S., please call, fax or e-mail us at info@bbks.com for the best-possible shipping rates.

Le bon de commande
order form

10 minutes a day® Series	QTY.	PRICE	TOTAL
ARABIC in 10 minutes a day®		$19.95	
CHINESE in 10 minutes a day®		$19.95	
FRENCH in 10 minutes a day®		$19.95	
GERMAN in 10 minutes a day®		$19.95	
HEBREW in 10 minutes a day®		$19.95	
INGLÉS en 10 minutos al día®		$19.95	
ITALIAN in 10 minutes a day®		$19.95	
JAPANESE in 10 minutes a day®		$19.95	
NORWEGIAN in 10 minutes a day®			
PORTUGUESE in 10 minutes a day®			
RUSSIAN in 10 minutes a day®			
SPANISH in 10 minutes a day®			

10 minutes a day		TOTAL
FRENCH		
FRENCH		
ITALIAN		
ITALIAN AUDIO		
SPANISH		
SPANISH AUDIO		

Language		TOTAL
ARABIC a language map®	$7.95	
CHINESE a language map®	$7.95	
FRENCH a language map®	$7.95	
GERMAN a language map®	$7.95	
GREEK a language map®	$7.95	
HAWAIIAN a language map®	$7.95	
HEBREW a language map®	$7.95	
INGLÉS un mapa del lenguaje®	$7.95	
ITALIAN a language map®	$7.95	
JAPANESE a language map®	$7.95	
NORWEGIAN a language map®	$7.95	
POLISH a language map®	$7.95	
PORTUGUESE a language map®	$7.95	
RUSSIAN a language map®	$7.95	
SPANISH a language map®	$7.95	
VIETNAMESE a language map®	$7.95	

Visit Bilingual Books, Inc. at: www.bbks.com for the latest list of titles and prices.

Item Total	
* Shipping	+
Total	
† Sales Tax	+
ORDER TOTAL	

† For delivery to individuals in Washington State, you must add 8.8% sales tax on the item total and the shipping costs combined. If your order is being delivered outside Washington State, you do not need to add sales tax.

Name _____

Address _____

_____

City _____ State _____ Zip _____

Day Phone (_____)_____

☐ My check or money order for $_____ is enclosed.
   Please make checks and money orders payable to Bilingual Books, Inc.

☐ Bill my credit card ☐ VISA ☐ MC ☐ AMEX
   No. _____ Exp. date ____/____
   Signature _____

Bilingual Books, Inc. • 1719 West Nickerson Street
Seattle, WA 98119 USA

10 minutes a day® AUDIO CD Series

by Kristine K. Kershul

The *10 minutes a day*® **AUDIO CD Series** is based on the immensely successful *10 minutes a day*® Series. Millions of people around the world have used the *10 minutes a day*® Series for over two decades.

• Eight hours of personal instruction on six CDs.

• Use the CDs in combination with the companion book, and maximize your progress as you see AND hear the language.

• Listen to native speakers and practice right along with them.

• Suitable for the classroom, the homeschooler, as well as business and leisure travelers.

• The CDs in the *10 minutes a day*® **AUDIO CD Series** may also be purchased separately from the *10 minutes a day*® books.

Language Map® Series

by Kristine K. Kershul

These handy *Language Maps*® provide the essential words and phrases to cover the basics for any trip.

• Over 1,000 essential words and phrases divided into convenient categories.

• Laminated , folding design allows for quicker reference while resisting spills, tearing, and damage from frequent use.

• Durable, to hold up to being sat on, dropped, and stuffed into backpacks, pockets, and purses.

• An absolute must for anyone traveling abroad or studying at home.

For a list of available languages and ordering information, please see the order form on the previous page.